TERRESTRIAL FISHING

TERRESTRIAL FISHING

The History and Development of the Jassid, Beetle, Cricket, Hopper, Ant, and Inchworm on Pennsylvania's Legendary Letort

by Ed Koch

Ed Koch

Foreword by Paul Schullery

Tying Sequence Illustrations by Rich Shires

Photographs by Norm Shires

Stackpole Books

Published by
STACKPOLE BOOKS
Cameron and Kelker Streets
P.O. Box 1831
Harrisburg, PA   17105

Printed in the United States of America

10 9 8 7 6 5 4 3 2 1

First edition

Book design by Art Unlimited.
Jacket design by Tracy Patterson.
Cover photo by Norm Shires.

Library of Congress Cataloging-in-Publication Data

Koch, Ed
    Terrestrial Fishing / by Ed Koch ; Foreword by Paul Schullery ; tying
  sequence illustrations by Rich Shires, photographs by Norm Shires.
  -- 1st Edition.
    p.   cm.
   ISBN 0-8117-0928-0
   1. Fly fishing. 2. Trout fishing. I. Title.
  SH451.K593   1989
   799.1'2--dc20   89-36114
                                                                      CIP

To Betty Ann,

for coming into my life at a critical time.

Contents

Acknowledgments   9

Foreword by Paul Schullery   11

Introduction   17

1 The Jassid   19

2 The Japanese Beetle   35

3 Ants   59

4 The Letort Hopper   83

5 The Cricket   101

6 Other Terrestrials   117

7 A Nine-Pounder   125

8 Tackle   137

9 Limestoners and Freestoners   143

10 Charles K. Fox: His Influence   161

Index   171

Acknowledgments

Sincere thanks to David Detweiler, Dianne Russell, Donna Pope, Marti Evans, and the entire Stackpole team for their confidence in this second work.

To Paul Schullery, a new friend and much admired writer, many thanks for the foreword. It cost me a dozen Letort Crickets in addition to several guided fishing trips. His advice, suggestions, and counseling have been invaluable.

Thanks to Norm Shires for his continued contributions of photographic talent. He just keeps getting better and better.

I'm grateful to Rich Shires for his pen-and-ink fly-tying illustrations.

Thanks also to: Charlie Fox for thirty years of friendship and tutelage; Rod and Deb Bond of Art Unlimited for their book design; Ed Sutrin for his McMurray Ant pattern; Frank Angelo, long-time friend, master fly tier and angler, for the Para-ant pattern; Jack Mickevicz of Jack's Tackle, a long-time friend in the business and too infrequent companion, for his Live Body Beetle, Ant, and Inchworm patterns; Mike Schell, of Mechanicsburg, Pennsylvania, one of Pennsylvania's finest young fly tiers, for his Grass Beetle pattern.

Foreword

Something in the Water

One of my favorite anecdotes from fly-fishing history is Vincent Marinaro's discovery of the tiny insect life on Letort Spring Run. This happened more than half a century ago. After yet another day of frustration with the creek's trout, he put aside his rod and simply lay down on the grass, absently staring at the stream. After a while his eyes began to focus on the surface film, and he noticed that there was something in the water. There were many somethings, in fact: hordes of tiny flies floating along all unbeknownst to him and his colleagues. That moment, that instant of insight, has taken its place among the foremost perceptual milestones of American fishing history. He would not be entitled to cry *Eureka!* for years—he still had to find a way to imitate those exasperatingly tiny things—but at once he knew what his challenge was, and that was a great part of the battle. It was a battle that, even then, Letort fishermen had been fighting for a long time.

The limestone country of south-central Pennsylvania is one of the true wellsprings of American fly fishing. Like Long Island and Cape Cod, the gentle farmlands around Harrisburg were popular among trout fishermen when the Adirondacks, the Catskills, the Poconos, and other famous eastern fishing grounds were still a sporting *terra incognita.*

For those who fish with an eye to the sport's traditions, a stream's historical personality is a lively and important part of the experience. When I took up fly fishing in 1972 and realized that it was going to be a lifetime pursuit, I made a short list of places I wanted to live: New England, Oregon, Alaska, and, perhaps foremost, south-central Pennsylvania. Now that I'm here I'm more impressed than ever with what these waters have to offer, not only in today's fishing but in a remarkable angling tradition.

A few history-minded fishermen know, for example, that fly fishermen were working the tricky currents and weed beds of the Letort as early as the 1790s. That's when George Gibson first fished there. Gibson, a native of Carlisle (the lovely little town through which the Letort flows) later became a distinguished U.S. Army general, but he is most important to anglers as one of our very first fly-fishing journalists. His articles on fishing the Letort, Big Spring, and other Pennsylvania streams began appearing in 1829, as soon as there was a sporting periodical to carry them.

Many more fishermen know of the great modern surge of fly-fishing innovation on these streams. Through the writings of Vincent Marinaro, Charles Fox, Ed Shenk, Sam Slaymaker, Ernest Schweibert, and a host of others, the area's contribution to twentieth-century angling has been studied and celebrated so that south-central Pennsylvania occupies a position in American fishing history since World War II much like that occupied by the Catskills before World War I. In neither case was one area responsible for all the new developments in fly fishing, but in both cases one area overflowed with new ideas and techniques that had a major impact on the direction of American fly fishing.

What with the greater intensity of fly-fishing travel, and the national and even international experience now available to any serious fly fisherman, it's less likely today that a single region could dominate fishing theory, as has happened in the past. The well-traveled angler is often the angler with the most opportunities to learn.

But there's a lot to be said for staying at home. Any thoughtful fisherman who concentrates on the streams near his home for half a lifetime or more is bound to notice different types of things than will the tourist who fishes everywhere on earth, once. Many of the greatest fly-fishing theorists of the past—Halford, Skues, Harding, Marinaro—were men of relatively limited geographical scope. There will always be a need for the ideas of the local fly fisher, the person who has learned one river so well that he can write about it in a way that is applicable to any trout water.

That quality of intimate familiarity—of having become at home with a stream—is one of the things that I have enjoyed most about the writings of the Letort regulars. Here were men who did not have a plane to catch tomorrow morning, who knew the patient joys of simply getting down on their bellies with their noses right on the current and just *watching* for an hour or two. They took the time to sit around—even installing a bench here and there along the stream—and talk about what they learned. From that level of attention to a stream's secrets comes a wisdom that the tourist/fisherman will never have. And out of that wisdom has come some of American fly fishing's most important conceptual leaps.

It is rarely possible to credit any one fisherman with originating anything alone. Almost all new developments grow out of older ones and are the products of cooperative effort. Thus it is with the Letort regulars. Read the stories in Marinaro's *A Modern Dry Fly Code*, or Fox's *This Wonderful World of Trout* and *Rising Trout*, and almost invariably you'll see that each new idea was the result of a day that started out with two or three guys going fishing together. There's lots of conversation, perhaps some arguing, often some laughs, and always some hard thinking. One of fishing's great joys is puzzling together over a problem.

Ed Koch has puzzled with the best of them. I've watched him catch some fish I never would have dreamed were catchable, and I don't hesitate to say that he *is* among the best of them himself. In the pantheon of Pennsylvania fishermen, he has earned his front-row seat (and I can hear him letting loose with a wide-eyed "Oh my gosh!" when he reads this; the trout here, and his own nature, have kept him humble about what he's achieved).

Ed has participated in the maturing of two great modern movements in fly fishing: midge fishing and terrestrials. His book *Fishing the Midge*, recently reissued to an appreciative and sizable audience, has for more than fifteen years been the standard guide to fishing tiny flies. The present book should occupy much the same position among terrestrial fishermen.

The imitation of terrestrials is not in itself a new idea. At least since the time of Walton and Cotton, anglers have observed, in print, that fish eat nonaquatic insects. In Cotton's immortal essay on "How to angle for trout or grayling in a clear stream," published as part of the 1676 edition of Walton's *Compleat Angler*, he recommended several terrestrial imitations. Among the twelve flies he recommended for June were a flying ant, a green grasshopper, and a small dun grasshopper. There were others recommended for that month that may also have been imitations of nonaquatic insects.

Many writers since then have included a few terrestrials in their list of flies: ants, grasshoppers, beetles, and an assortment of what some of them called *pismires* all got some attention. Alfred Ronalds's great book, *The Fly-Fisher's*

Entomology, first published in 1836, is now regarded as the work that brought British angling entomology into the modern era; it included ants, caterpillars, a beetle, and other obviously land-based insects. As the eighteenth century progressed, both British and American writers added more terrestrial imitations to their lists, but the flies did not become a major part of the fly fisher's arsenal until more recently. Fishermen in various parts of the country experimented with terrestrials, but it was left to the Letort regulars to turn experimentation into a movement.

Now that I've read the manuscript, I'm glad to be able to say that this isn't an encyclopedic guide to all the terrestrial imitations ever invented anywhere. Ed has fished widely (one of the first times I heard of him was when he was conducting seminars for Bud Lilly in Montana in the early 1970s), and he mentions some of those faraway experiences here when it's helpful to do so, but this book is in the tradition of the earlier works from the Letort regulars. Marinaro, Fox, and others wrote about the fishing they knew, and they made it easy for readers to understand how to apply those lessons to any trout waters. I read this manuscript with a growing excitement as I recognized how well *Terrestrial Fishing* fits into that tradition. You will enjoy Ed's many fishing stories, but when you finish a chapter you'll realize that, even if the stories all involve Pennsylvania, the lessons have universal application. When he describes how Ed Shenk tied the wing flat over the body of the Letort Hopper, he is explaining the effectiveness of any number of later hopper imitations that work on the same principle. When he tells how easy it was to mistake a rise to ants for a rise to a hatch of Tricos, he's telling fishermen everywhere not to be too sure of themselves. When he demonstrates that something works on the Yellow Breeches, he is telling us something that will be of value on tough trout waters everywhere, and of singular value on the dozens of spring creeks in other parts of the country.

I'm also glad as a fishing historian, because Ed has saved many important episodes here, encounters with the other exceptional fishermen he's known on these streams. Here are many of the most important moments in recent fly-fishing history, from the memory of a key participant. Ed's long involvement in the development of terrestrials gives this book a degree of authenticity, of firsthandedness, that makes for exciting reading.

His book appeals to me on another, more subjective, level as well. Ed Koch writes with a level of companionableness that seems to be a common trait among the Pennsylvania fishing writers. When I read many of our other master anglers I have the feeling that The Word is coming down to me from on high. No doubt many of these writers are entitled to feel technically superior to most of us who fish, but I'd just as soon not have to wade through the condescension to get the information.

But when I read Marinaro, or Fox, or Grove, or Koch, or any of the other famous Pennsylvanians, I somehow feel part of a conversation—a lively, opinionated, and friendly dialogue. Whatever type of personality they may have had (part of Vincent Marinaro's legend hereabouts is his crankiness), however varied their writing styles, they communicated with warmth and in a hearty spirit of inquiry. There writers seem more sympathetic and at ease about what they know than many others. I don't know why it should be that way. Maybe it's something in the water.

Paul Sch·illery
Hershey, Pennsylvania

Introduction

It was with great hesitation (perhaps uncertainty is more accurate) that I mentioned the possibility of a terrestrial book to Dianne Russell at Stackpole Books after the revised second edition of *Fishing the Midge* had been completed. I felt strongly that this story should be told, perhaps by Vince Marinaro, Charlie Fox, Ed Shenk, or even Joe Brooks or Ernie Schweibert. Vince, Charlie, and Ed were active participants in the development, testing, and trying of the terrestrial patterns. I, on the other hand, was fortunate indeed to have been involved, but only as an active angler.

When I moved to Carlisle, Pennsylvania, in 1957, I had no idea what lay ahead for me over the next thirty years. What transpired was an experience that few anglers are ever privileged to have. I met such men as Charlie Fox, Ed Shenk, Vince Marinaro, Ernie Schweibert, Ernie Hille, Joe Brooks, Don Dubois, Sam Slaymaker, Lefty Kreh, Ross Trimmer, Ed Zern, Tap Tappley, Ted Williams, William Conrad, Lee Wulff, Ben Schley, Wes Jordan, Leon Chandler, Dick Wood, Eric Peper, and dozens of other well-known fly fishermen.

What amazed me (and still does) was their openness and willingness to share whenever they could. This was not some kind of special treatment I received, they were that way with everyone—regular and visitor alike.

Whatever has happened to me or has taken place in my angling career has been a direct result of what I have learned from others and what others have done for me. It is for that reason that I wanted to tell this story, as well as to pass on a bit of the fly-fishing history that took place in Carlisle and the Cumberland Valley.

The Jassid

It was during the late 1940s and early 1950s that two Carlisle-area anglers, who literally lived on and regularly fished the limestone waters of the Cumberland Valley, intensified their investigations into the surface-feeding activities of free-rising browns (trout who rise all day long to no apparent hatch). Charlie Fox and Vince Marinaro had been studying the trout, their feeding habits, and the insects of the Letort for many years. Their experiences had been frustrating, to say the least. Conventional flies, presentations, and methods were ignored time after time, day after day, week after week. They would sit by the hour and watch a surface-feeding "regular" rise consistently but could not discover what the trout was taking. There were no hatches in progress and nothing visible on the water's surface. Still, the trout continued to feed.

Only after exhausting every conceivable method of discovery—including lying on their stomachs, their faces only inches from the water's surface, scanning the current in a trout's feeding lane in an effort to see something, anything, on or in the water—did they decide on screening. They held their nets (very fine pieces of cloth attached to wooden dowel rods) behind a feeding trout where the current would carry whatever it was the trout was taking to their waiting traps. Examination revealed all kinds of minute "things" crawling and clinging to the nets, but not the usual aquatic insects they expected to find and for which they had really been looking. Instead, their collection revealed myriad land-bred insects—leafhoppers, ants, beetles, woodworms—*terrestrials*. Could this be what these wild stream-bred trout were taking on the surface? The only logical conclusion to be drawn was that, indeed, this array of land-bred bugs had to be it. The only thing left for Charlie and Vince to do was prove their theory. Well, the rest is history related in Vince's *A Modern Dry Fly Code*, and Charlie's *This Wonderful World of Trout*.

In the early 1950s Joe Brooks was Fishing Editor of *Outdoor Life*, and in a kickoff article introduced Vince's and Charlie's find to the American angler. Joe fished the Jassids and proved their effectiveness beyond any doubt. Across the United States and in trout waters in many other countries the results were always the same. When Joe used the limestoner's Jassid—success!

Originally the flies were tied in sizes 16 to 24. Today, with the availability of size 26 and 28 hooks, the Jassid has been made even more effective. They are tied on fine-wire hooks. The patterns vary from black to brown to gray to yellow to green. The flies are relatively easy to tie (we will get into tying at the end of this chapter). Even a beginner with just a little practice can put together a Jassid that will take trout.

The Jassid was fished differently from any other pattern

that had been tied or fished in the area. It opened up more potential to the local anglers than they had ever dreamed possible. It was to radically change fishing on the limestone and freestone waters in Pennsylvania. To this day, I don't think there has been anything to equal it.

Some of the stories connected with the early times and development of the patterns are quite humorous. Vince and Charlie, of course, before all the publicity on the Jassid had gotten out, were quite busy getting solid results and trying to find out for sure if this was the answer to their unsolved problem. Each time they went on the Letort they had their fly boxes full of Jassids. They would keep track of how many trout they found feeding and how many they could fool into taking, whether they hooked them or missed them, and how many could be deceived with the new patterns.

Some of the regulars had no idea what was happening. They would see Vince and Charlie on the stream and notice during the middle of the day that they were rising trout, were catching trout, and were having much more success than the regulars themselves. Charlie and Vince were very secretive about the whole experiment. Whenever one of them got hooked in a tree or weeds, they were sometimes unable to find the hung-up flies. The regulars, who were sitting and watching from the bushes, would go down and scour the area for hours trying to find out what Vince and Charlie were using. Well, some of them found out, and I can remember many evenings talking to Norm Lightner about the hide-and-seek episodes. When Norm and others finally found the Jassid, the word spread and the fly soon became as popular as hot dogs and hamburgers.

The techniques and approach were, of course, much different from those that had previously been used. Technique continued to be worked out for ten years or more by many notable anglers who fished the Letort: Don Dubois, Ernie Schweibert, Ross Trimmer, Ed Shenk, Norm Lightner, Frank Honisch, and others.

To fish the Jassids in those days (about 1956, I think), the first part of the approach was to watch the stream and look for free-rising trout. Once you located your trout, the best thing to do was just to sit and watch, to learn how regularly he rose and whether he rose in the same spot every time, where the current was bringing the naturals to him. Casting styles were a little bit different as the Jassid techniques were being refined. Long leaders had to be used. Tippets in those days were usually 5X, 6X, or 7X. Today 8X is available and some material even goes down to three-quarter-pound test.

Most of the casting to the Jassid feeders was done from a downstream position so that the fly drifted to the trout with as little drag as possible. More often than not the trout were found close to the banks, lying under the overhanging grass where the insects fell in good quantity into the water. Casting had to be very accurate. The fly had to be thrown a foot or more in front of the feeding trout with enough slack in the leader so that, as the artificial drifted toward the fish, it wouldn't drag. It required a great deal of skill, a lot of practice, and perhaps more than anything else, a lot of luck. One nice thing about the new pattern was that the yellow jungle-cock eye used for the Jassid was more visible floating down in the surface film than many of the standard patterns used before had been.

The approach to the trout was different. Once you located a fish in a feeding position and you were twenty or thirty yards downstream, you had to be very careful not to get too close and spook him. A shadow thrown on the water or the heavy step of a boot on the bank would often send the trout

out of their feeding stations into the safety of the weeds. When you located your fish you had to crawl on your hands and knees, keeping a low silhouette, to get into casting position. Often, it would take fifteen minutes or more to get into position to cast.

One of the early anglers on the Letort whose memory will be with me as long as I fish or even thing of fishing, was Frank Honisch of Philadelphia. Frank would drive to Carlisle every other weekend. He would arrive at the house about 6:00 or 6:30 a.m., have a cup of coffee, and then be off to the Letort. He would fish from early morning until dark. I have never seen anyone fish as hard or with such intensity as Frank did on the Letort in those days. He considered it a good day when he was able to catch trout in the double digits. Any day under ten he thought of as poor. Quite frequently after the first season he had many double-numbered days.

I can remember sitting back watching him as he located trout after trout, fishing from Charlie Fox's meadow up to the quarry bridge. He would locate a trout, sit and watch him, then slowly but surely work himself into position. Frank was always very certain where he had to be positioned, where his fly would have to be, where the line of drift was, and where the trout would take. He had everything down to a science. He would crawl on his hands and knees into position and lay out one or two false casts about ten feet or so to the free side of the trout. This was to be sure he had the distance and knew just where his fly would land. When he felt everything was ready, up came the fly off the water and the cast was made. Frank was one of the few men I have ever seen who could take and release almost every trout he fished over in a day. It was pure pleasure to watch him work those tiny Jassids.

For a long while in the late fifties the Jassid fishing was confined primarily to the Letort and the Big Spring. Then one day Dick Wood came to fish and he wanted to try the Yellow Breeches. We started at the upper end of the fly area. Dick liked to fish downstream. He would start off with nymphs and if there wasn't much action he would bring out his dry flies at the first sign of surface-feeding activity. On this particular morning I followed Dick downstream. Tight against the bank, he was rising, missing, or catching trout on almost every cast. For every trout he rose, it took me half a dozen casts before one would show even half-hearted interest in my imitation. In desperation I asked Dick what he was using. "Oh, just some of your Jaspers," was his reply. He called them "Jaspers" in jest, I'm sure. Sometimes, however, he left one with the feeling that perhaps this pattern was just another passing fancy, one that wouldn't stand the test of time.

In spite of what his real thoughts about the fly were, he could use it on the Breeches and raise trout after trout after trout. He fished tight against the far bank, which was more than troublesome, to say the least. You couldn't wade the middle because of the depth and swiftness of the current. So casting had to be done across the rapidly moving middle water to get your fly to the far side, sometimes just inches from the bank. You had to have enough slack when the line landed on the water to give the fly a drift of a foot or so to reach the trout. Watching Dick manipulate his line in the fast-flowing current to get his #18 Jassid in front of the bank-feeding trout taught me tactics that I will use in terrestrial fishing for the rest of my life.

Spring Creek, at Bellefonte, Pennsylvania, provided another testing ground for the Jassid. Long established as a "regulated" area, it was a favorite of mid- and late-summer fly fishers. There was plenty of long flat water with channels of weeds that harbored dozens and dozens of trout—surface-feeding trout that seemed to be there only to test the ability of the angler. From midsummer on the trout would lie just inches beneath the surface and feed constantly, even though nothing was visible on the water.

Fishing the Jassids with 6X or 7X revealed for the first time that these choosy surface feeders could be fooled, and not just the occasional fish, but as many as a dozen or more in a stretch. But casts had to be right on the money. As long as the fly drifted in the trout's feeding lane, drag free, he usually took. Fishing the fly slightly upstream from behind the trout was the most productive position. Leaders of ten or twelve feet soon became necessary because any time a fly line was visible in the trout's window meant a refusal, and more often than not a spooked trout.

Wanting to try the Jassids on water that I could be fairly certain hadn't been fished, I traveled to nearby Maryland and a little-known (at that time) limestoner called Beaver Creek. Lefty Kreh introduced me to it some twenty years ago. Back then Beaver Creek wasn't pounded hard except for a few weeks in the early part of the season when the state stocked. It held a good population of streambred browns as finicky at times as any of our Pennsylvania limestone trout. It was very much like the Letort, though smaller in size. Full of cress and elodea, it was an ideal spot to give the Jassid a real try.

Parking in a secluded area Lefty had shown me on one of our trips, I assembled my rod and donned hip boots, vest, and glasses. I checked an assortment of Jassids, tied on a 7X leader with a #20 black-hackled pattern, and after a cup of coffee from the thermos, was off to the stream. I kept well back from the bank so as not to disturb any trout that might be out in feeding stations, all the while scanning the surface for the familiar ring of a rising brown on the way downstream. After I covered about four hundred yards, the stream revealed a dozen or more risers. "Probably more than that up," I thought, "in close to my side of the grass." It was late June and there weren't any signs that anyone had been by in days.

Stopping just where the meadow ended and a wooded stretch began, I edged to the bank on my knees, looking for trout. Sure enough, in the middle of the stream in an open channel of the weeds, two trout were casually dimpling the surface. I didn't know for sure if there were leafhoppers on the water, but one thing *was* certain—there were plenty of them in the meadow grass.

Working out line with false casts and laying the fly some five feet or more to the trout's left to be sure the distance was right, checking the drift of the current, and figuring everything was okay, I lifted the tiny imitation from the water, made a few false casts, and let it go for its mark. The fly landed about eighteen inches above the trout. The leader was curled just enough so that there wouldn't be any drag problem. I lifted the rod tip and mended line as the fly approached the trouts' window; the first trout rose, nose under the fly, looked, inspected, and drifted back with it. After what seemed an eternity, though it was only a matter of seconds, his mouth opened and the tiny terrestrial disappeared. The rod tip rose abruptly, the hook bit home, and off raced the trout for the cover of the weeds. Immediately the second trout spooked, but it didn't matter—the Jassid's first try on foreign water was successful. Up and down the tiny channel the trout fought, trying to shake the biting hook. Slowly, he slid over the weeds to net: a plump ten-inch brownie. I released him, cleaned and dried the fly, and looked upstream to locate another riser.

Ten or fifteen yards upstream and in close to the far bank came the familiar ring of another rise. About a thirty-foot cast would be needed if I was lucky enough to be able to crawl upstream and get behind a clump of grass for cover. There were some weeds about midstream, so it would be difficult to get a drag-free float. Slowly I crawled upstream, watching the trout rise every fifteen seconds or so, which was a good indication that a steady flow of food was being carried to him. False-cast a few times, shoot the line, and drop the fly about four feet to the trout's left was the repeat pattern. The range was good. "Quick current, fast drag, so allow a little more slack in the line," ran through my mind as the tiny fly lifted from the surface. Again the line and fly shot for the target. The fly landed in the grass on the far bank. Quickly, before the leader had a chance to hit the water, drag, and spook the trout, I raised the rod tip and freed the fly. The second cast was better. It landed about two feet in front of the rising brown with enough slack in the leader not to drag. Down along the edge of the grass the fly danced on the surface, in and out, in and out, floating freely in the current. When the fly was within eight inches of the trout he saw it, was up under it, and without a second's hesitation opened his mouth and inhaled the tiny fooler. *Strike.* Off shot trout number two toward the center channel and through the weeds. A few minutes later I turned an eleven-inch brownie back.

Twenty yards or so upstream another trout was feeding, again in a midstream channel in the weeds. Figuring this was going to be a real easy one, I laid the first cast to the trout. The leader hit just on his head and away he shot, down into the cover of the channel. "What a crazy mistake," I muttered to myself. Picking the fly off the water and reeling in line, I began to look upstream for more trout. Upstream about thirty yards there was a tangle of limbs in the water. Fortunately, the current broke to the left side of the debris and carried an abundance of food to a channel or pocket in the weed. There was a good-sized trout working.

Remembering what happened just a few minutes before and deciding to really play this one safe, I false-cast several times, making sure the distance was just right. The fly would have to land just ahead of the limbs and be carried naturally by the current to the left in order to fool the trout. The cast was perfect. Around the corner of the pocket came the Jassid. Up came the trout from his feeding station. Hesitating for a few seconds, he began to drift backward under the tiny imitation. Just before the fly was ready to float out of his pocket, his nose broke the surface. Gills flared ever so slightly, typical of Letort browns. The fly disappeared in the ring. This one turned out to be a brown of about thirteen inches.

The rest of the day was a repeat of the first hour or so of morning fishing. I raised some fifteen trout, missed some but hooked more in about four hours of fishing. "Pretty good test for this new fly on water that more than likely hasn't seen any of the imitation Jassids," I mused.

The Jassid was really working well and had more than proved itself on the limestone waters where there was an abundance of terrestrials. I couldn't help but wonder what it might do on freestone streams or a small mountain brook. Would it be as effective there?

A few weeks later I drove to Maryland again to fish Big Hunting Creek, a small, tumbling mountain stream just above Thurmont. At that time it was flies-only, but trout could be kept and it was fished rather heavily.

Parking at the ranger station, I readied my gear, slipped

on hip boots, had a quick cup of coffee, and headed for the stream. There were several long, quiet pools, under overarching trees, that always held trout that would lie in the shadows near the bank. After approaching the first pool, I stood back and watched. There were a few trout rising. Scanning the water with the Polaroids, I could see a dozen or more trout in feeding stations.

I walked downstream, waded into the riffle below the pool, and eased my way into the tail of the long, quiet, flat stretch. There were two trout feeding against the righthand bank, facing upstream. Getting down on my knees in the shallow water to allow more overhead casting room, I worked out line. False-casting several times, I let the fly go toward the middle of the stream, away from the trout so as not to spook them, to insure I had the proper distance. After carefully picking the fly off I cast with a slight right-hand curve, placing the Jassid under the overhanging limbs into the quiet, still water near the edge. Slowly the leader drifted downstream, pulling the tiny imitation toward me. As it approached the first trout I could see it was too far off to his left. I did not pick it off the water but let it ride the slow current. It came into the feeding lane of the last trout in the tail of the pool. Up he came, and without any hesitation jumped on top of the little Jassid and headed for the bank. The hook held, the tippet held, and in a few minutes a plump eight-inch rainbow glided into the net.

Releasing the trout, I lit my pipe and let the pool settle down, watching upstream for feeding activity. After a few minutes, about thirty feet upstream two trout near the middle of the pool, where the overhanging limbs reached out the farthest, began to feed. Slowly I eased my way forward, being careful not to send any disturbing ripples ahead of me. Getting into position, I false-cast and let the Jassid fall to the trout nearest midstream. It floated down, he rose, again without any hesitation, and took the imitation. He was about the same size as trout number one.

I couldn't help wondering if this was just luck or if the Jassid would really be as effective on freestone streams as it had been on the limestoners. Letting the pool quiet down, I watched for the trout to resume feeding. Sure enough, before long they started again. This time they were in near the bank, under the limbs. I cast again to the trout nearest me. The cast landed just right. The trout drifted over slightly to his left, looked at the fly, and took. I guess I was a little tense. "Struck too soon and missed the trout. He won't come back for a while," I mumbled to myself while slowly edging upstream.

The next trout lay just behind a submerged rock, about a third of the way in from the righthand bank. I placed the fly slightly to his left. It drifted down past the rock and into his feeding lane. Up he came, and took. The rod tip rose. He shot for the bank, then turned and headed downstream. The tiny tippet did its job. A few minutes later I released a nice ten-inch rainbow.

After checking the fly to make sure the hook was all right, the barb intact, and the jungle-cock eye not split or broken, I resumed watching the water toward the head of the pool. About four more trout were still feeding. Without moving, I cast to the nearest trout. He rose to the fly like it was something he had been anxiously awaiting. It was an eleven-inch brown, unusual for this stream because the state stocked mostly rainbows in those days.

On my way to the head of the pool I raised and missed two more trout, hooked one more and released it. I fished several hundred yards of water in the next few hours. Pools, riffles, and broken water, and always the story was the

Terrestrial Fishing

same: the trout took the Jassid as if they hadn't eaten in a week. It was gratifying, to say the least, that the new imitation worked so well on freestone waters. Evidently, the trout were used to looking for and feeding on landbred insects as well as mayflies, just as the trout of the meadow streams did.

For myself as well as for many of the limestone regulars, the Jassid proved to be a boon over the years. Had it not been for this new pattern, many days would have been troutless.

Some years later the federal government banned the importation of the jungle cock. Those fly tiers who were fortunate enough to have some jungle-cock necks on hand produced flies for a few years. By the early 1970s there were almost no Jassids available with natural jungle-cock eyes. A few years later Eric Leiser, now of the Fly Fisherman's Bookcase, brought to the market imitation jungle cock. At first most fly tiers (including me) were skeptical that anything could take the place of natural jungle cock. Even so, we tried them. I tied flies down to #22 with them. Sometimes you had to trim the imitation eye to make it fit the size of the hook, but it worked. So, for those of you who are perhaps just getting into fly fishing, or who have heard about the Jassids and have not been able to obtain any commercially, don't be afraid to try some of the plastic imitations. They do work, and quite well.

The Jassid is not a difficult fly to tie. On the contrary, it is one of the easier patterns to produce.

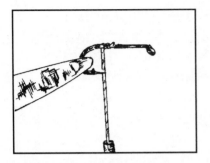

1. Secure hook in vise and attach tying thread above hook point.

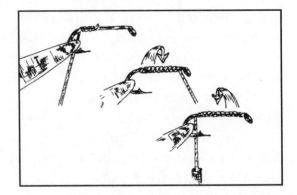

2. Wrap thread back on shank to the point at which the hook begins to bend. Wrap thread forward on shank stopping just in front of the hook eye. Wrap back again to the rear of the hook shank.

Tying the Jassid

Hook: Sizes #18 to #28 (Mustad 94833, Tiemco 101)

Thread: Black, brown, green, yellow, or orange

Body: Same as thread

Hackle: Same as thread

Wing: Imitation jungle-cock eye

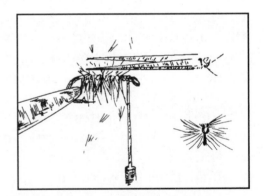

5. Clip a "V" in top of the hackle.

6. Wrap thread to the hook eye and back to the point where the hackle was tied off. (This step is important because it builds up a small hump that the stem of the jungle-cock eye is tied down to. The hump will be slightly

3. Tie in hackle by the stem or butt section.

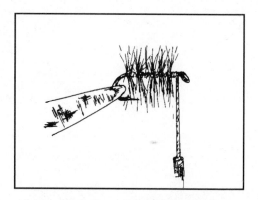

4. Wrap hackle palmer-style over body, stopping where the thread stops, just in front of the hook eye. Clip off hackle tip.

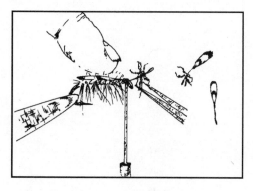

higher than the "V" clipped in the hackle, thus preventing the eye from popping or sticking up in the air when the tying thread is pulled tight.) With the right hand, pick up the eye, stem-first, and lay it on top of the hook shank. The eye will be lying flat along the hook with the rounded part toward the bend of the hook. Hold the eye flat in position with the thumb of the left hand, if you're a right-handed tier (obviously, your hands will be reversed if you tie left-handed). Tie down the stem of the eye.

7. Wrap the head of the fly, going forward and backward several times to make sure all the plastic is covered. Whip-finish, clip excess thread, apply head cement, and the fly is complete.

The Japanese Beetle

The success of the Jassid pattern was only the beginning. The knowledge that trout feed eagerly on terrestrials opened up an entirely new area of fly-tying possibilities.

One such pattern was the Japanese Beetle. These beetles were abundant in unbelievable numbers along the meadows of the Letort in the late 1950s and early 1960s. Wild rose bushes, honeysuckle, and mulberry trees made a literal haven for trout food. Vince and Charlie soon found out that the trout loved the beetles as well as they did the leafhopper, or Jassid. The trout would take the beetles as eagerly, if not more so, as mayflies during some of the heavier hatches that occurred during those years.

The discovery of the terrestrials led to new fishing experiences. One didn't have to wait for the few hatching mayflies to start the trout rising. Almost any time during the day the possibility that leafhoppers or beetles might be on the water was excellent.

I'm not sure who tied the first beetle pattern. Whether it

was Charlie, Vince, Ernie Schweibert, Don Dubois, or Ed Shenk, they all enjoyed much success during those first days of the new pattern.

Some of my discussions with Charlie have led me to believe that Ernie tied the pattern that was most successful in the early years. It was tied with a black dubbed body or black thread body, black hackle, and green head feathers from a ring-necked pheasant rooster for the wing. The wing made of the iridescent green ring-neck feather was probably one of the most unique innovations ever to be used in fly tying. The feathers were matched in pairs, cemented together with head cement, and laid on waxed paper to dry. The head cement made the wing of the fly more durable during casting and trout taking. The wings had to be shaped with scissors to fit the size of the hook used. For a long time most of the avid fly tiers in the Cumberland Valley of Pennsylvania had all their hunting friends saving ring-neck heads for them to tie flies with over the winter.

Some of the early stories about practices that took place along the Letort and especially with the Japanese Beetles will no doubt surprise some readers. I would like to relate some of these tales because they are a part of the history of the development of the terrestrials. There is a tremendous amount to be learned from the experiences of Charlie, Vince, and the other Letort regulars.

One of the things we did early in the game was to chum with live beetles. Now don't forget, this was long before there was any regulated water in Pennsylvania. And before you throw up your hands and cry "for shame," read on.

In the early 1950s Charlie and Vince had instituted their own regulation of releasing trout. Way back then you were permitted to catch and keep two trout fourteen inches or better; all others had to be returned to the water. Barbless

Terrestrial Fishing

hooks also were required. Most local and visiting anglers were more than happy to abide by these regulations because they knew that when they fished the Letort they would find rising trout to fish over. So don't knock the beetle-feeding as some kind of unsportsmanlike or underhanded method of angling. It was far from that!

What we used to do was to set beetle traps. The beetles were a nuisance to people who lived closed to the stream because they loved rose bushes, flowers, and shrubs. Residents were glad to see at least some of the beetles disappear. So traps were set, and when you went to fish the Letort and were one of those who knew about the traps, you were welcome to go up, empty the beetles from the trap into a jar or container, and head for the stream and some fun (or frustration, depending on how you looked at the end results of your day). You were required to reset the trap so more beetles would be available for the next angler or photographer.

The procedure was to walk upstream to a special area in the meadow and throw a handful of beetles into the water. As they floated downstream in the current you watched for the trout to begin rising. On a good day in a stretch of perhaps fifty yards, you might have a half dozen or more trout begin to feed on the floating beetles. You could, after much practice, pinpoint the feeding location of the trout in that particular stretch of water. You would then walk downstream, away from the bank, and begin to work the water with an artificial beetle. Now, this may seem like a pretty easy undertaking, but believe me, it was far from that. You could cast and cast and cast, get a perfect float or drift time after time over those beetle-eating browns, and if you were lucky, you might—after working half a dozen trout—hook and land one!

Remember, these were streambred browns, not stocked trout. They had never been fed artificially, and I firmly believe that the beetle chumming was not artificial to them. I would guess that at times, in a high wind or when the cows or horses pushed through the bushes near the stream's edge, as many beetles were knocked into the water, if not more, than we ever threw in by hand. So, although we thought we were creating some kind of artificial hatch, I still wonder to this day if we really were.

I would venture to say that, after several seasons of this, a good number of the surface feeders were hooked a few times each. We kept track of these trout: where they fed, where they dashed for cover when spooked, and where they sought protection when hooked. It was all part of a new learning experience for us. Occasionally, some of the fish were fin-clipped or tagged. This enabled us to keep track of particular trout season after season, especially if they moved, from year to year, to new or safer locations or better feeding stations.

Well, I suppose one might think that with all this feeding, finding, and observing the same trout over and over, it was rather easy to win at our little game. Nothing could be further from the truth. Those crazy trout would feed at will, but seldom succumbed to the angler's hook. They would rise to the artificials time after time and refuse at the last minute. I'm sure it was not always the fly or pattern. You had drag with which to contend and the Letort probably has more shifting and varying currents in ten feet of water than any other stream in the world. Not to mention weeds, grass, limbs, and a variety of other frustrating obstacles found on no other stream. Needless to say, casting technique and fly presentation became a more integral part of our Letort fishing than did the fly patterns.

Speaking of fly patterns, you have never seen nor could you ever imagine some of the patterns that were to be found dangling from the tippets of the regulars for several seasons. If my memory of talks with Charlie serves me correctly, Vince's first beetle was tied with a coffee bean. That's right, a coffee bean. The bean was flat on the bottom, oval-shaped, and round on top—just the shape of the Japanese Beetle. Vince cut a groove in the bottom or flat side in order to be able to glue it to the hook shank. Black hackle was palmered up the shank of the hook and the top of the hackle was clipped off; a V was clipped in the underside of the hackle. The coffee bean was then glued to the hook shank. The fly really looked like a beetle. The size, shape, silhouette, and color were just right. I'm not so sure how easy it was to cast or control. By the time I met Charlie and Vince, they had gone on to newer and better patterns.

Don Dubois was another who tried all kinds of beetle patterns. Even after the pheasant-feather imitation was being used, Don was still searching for the perfect beetle. He was that kind of guy, never satisfied and always searching for the ultimate. As long as I fish, I will never forget one of the wildest patterns he made, though I must admit it was fairly productive. Don called it a "Flure." It was a combination of a fly and a lure and was made with a type of sheet foam rubber. Don would cut the oval beetle shape from the rubber. Sometimes he would wind hackle on the hook shank, sometimes not, and then tie or glue the oval foam on top just as Vince did the coffee bean. This fly was much lighter in weight and easier to cast. It floated well and was almost indestructible. Many of the regulars scoffed at it and wouldn't try it because it wasn't made of fur and feather, but in spite of this it did work. Don would sit by the hour in the meadow making beetles for anyone who wanted one.

Don was messing with the rubber flies during the years 1960 to 1962—over twenty-five years ago. Today every mail-order catalog in the country sells foam-rubber body material for beetles, ants, and inchworms. Ironic quirk of fate, isn't it?

Whenever someone new showed up on the stream, he would inevitably meet Charlie Fox. Charlie became known as "the gentleman host of the Letort." He would spend hours acquainting the newcomer with the better stretches of the stream. He showed them where trout lived and fed, as well as what flies to use and when to use them.

Without fail, Charlie would tell of the beetle-feeding. I know many who thought he was perhaps pulling their legs. When asked if they wanted to try the feeding technique, all would accept: some, I'm sure, because they felt it would be an easy way to take a trout on such storied water; others, perhaps, because they did not want to offend their gracious host. Nevertheless, all who visited the Letort and were invited to try for the beetle-feeders did just that.

Upstream the newcomer was led by Charlie to one of the beetle traps. The trap was emptied, the jar replaced, and then off they'd go to some stretch of the river that held a good number of trout. They would kneel in the grass as a handful of beetles was thrown on the water. Within minutes the first trout would come up and gulp, gulp, gulp. The beetles began to disappear. Then another would start, and another and another, until there might be six or eight trout feeding along the floating line of beetles.

Without fail, this was enough to excite the most skeptical of visitors. I doubt that any of them had ever seen that many rising trout in such a short stretch of water. It was difficult for them to contain themselves without first being asked to go ahead and try for the risers. Ninety percent of them were so excited that they put down the entire string of feeders with the first cast. This, in spite of the fact that they were well coached on what to do and how to do it. You never saw such exasperated, frustrated, and dumbfounded fly fishers in your life. Those who were able to settle down and control themselves usually did a little better as the day went on. Others were never able to calm themselves enough to catch even the first trout.

Back on the bench in Charlie's meadow after an hour or so, it was always the same. "What happened?" "How did I spook all those fish?" "My casting was terrible." "How do you do it?" "I've never experienced anything like it in my life." On and on they would ramble and mutter to themselves and to Charlie, or whomever it was that had taken them on the guided tour. For some of them you had to feel sorry. For others it was difficult not to laugh. Had we only taken movies, they would be priceless today. A few were able to catch trout and really understand what was taking place along those waters. Those few would spend hours talking with the regulars about the trout, their feeding habits, the water, casting techniques, patterns, and the newfound challenge of the terrestrials.

As I mentioned earlier, many patterns were tied and tried: ring-neck rooster feathers, mallard breast feathers, grouse feathers, quail feathers—anything that could be made to give the shape of the Japanese Beetle. You must remember that these insects floated in the surface film of the water. They did not ride up high like the mayfly, but made a different silhouette and light pattern for the trout to see.

As I mentioned, the best pattern was of green cock-pheasant feathers because it looked almost black. It gave the best silhouette, when viewed from underneath, of the actual shape of the real beetle. The palmered hackle imitated the legs and the trimmed feather looked exactly like the real beetle when viewed from the bottom. One problem with it was that it was very delicate. Even though the feathers had been glued together and trimmed to size, you had to cut the stem very narrow in order to tie it on the hook shank. Wherever you tied the feather down and wrapped the thread back to make the head of the fly, the feather or wing would eventually crack or break at that point. Sometimes it was in casting when the wing would fly off, or it would break when you hooked a trout. No matter. Once that wing cracked, that was the end of the fly.

Many fly tiers tried to solve the problem with all kinds of hard-to-imagine patterns. I'm not certain who first tied it, but Ed Shenk was the first one to let me in on the secret of the clipped-deer-hair beetle. This fly was tied with black deer hair. The hair was packed on the hook and flared, just as in making a deer-hair bass bug or muddler head. It was trimmed flat on the bottom, oval on the sides, and round on top. It looked great, floated like a cork, and was indestructible. It is probably the most popular beetle pattern even today.

So much for some of the early stories and the development of beetle patterns. At the end of this period, in the early 1960s, the Letort had been written about in every major fishing magazine, and on weekends fishing pressure was becoming heavy. Gone were the Saturdays and Sundays on which you could pick a stretch or two in the meadow and fish to and observe trout for a couple of hours, undisturbed by anything but an occasional cow coming down from the meadow to drink or cool off.

By this time, the fly stretch had been open on the Yellow Breeches for some years; however, it wasn't fished nearly as heavily as the Letort was. When I wanted to try some new

Terrestrial Fishing

patterns or get away from the crowd and have a few rising trout to myself, I would head out to the Yellow Breeches. Just above the dam at Allenberry, and above the big white house along the bank, there was a stretch of deep quiet water. The banks were lined with trees, wild rose bushes, and all kinds of flowers that made excellent beetle cover. To my surprise the area abounded in Japanese beetles. You could walk along and see trout lying within six inches of the bank, back under the cover of the brush, just feeding away on the helpless beetles as they hit the water.

The water was quite deep here and, as mentioned, not too many anglers were fishing this section because the only way to get a fly on the water was from the bank. It was heavily overgrown and difficult to cast from. In front of the big white house above Allenberry were the remains of a mill dam that had been there for many years. A rock wall about two feet under the surface stretched from one bank to the other. You could walk out on the wall and, once you reached the middle of the stream, wade upstream or down for perhaps fifty or seventy yards. There were some huge buttonwood trees right at the dam that were full of beetles. On numerous occasions this stretch provided me with hours of undisturbed fishing with the new beetle patterns.

One Sunday morning I went down, sat on the bench, and watched the water. There must have been a dozen-and-a-half trout rising in an area of less than seventy-five yards, all under the overhanging branches of the buttonwoods. Taking one of the clipped-deer-hair beetles in a size #14, I tied it to a 6X tippet and walked down to the edge of the bank, over the wall, and into the water. Slowly I edged my way up to the old mill dam. Just a few feet in front of the wall three trout were feeding in a ten-foot circle. It was difficult casting because the limbs hung almost to within four feet of the water's edge. I had to cast sidearm in order to get my line and fly up under the limbs to the feeding trout.

As I watched the trout closest to me, he rose. I couldn't see any beetles on the water; I couldn't really see *anything* on the water. I was fairly certain, though, that the trout were taking some sort of landbred insects that were falling from the buttonwoods, perhaps an ant or small beetle or some kind of woodworm. False-casting, trying to get the right distance, I laid the fly about ten feet to the left of the trout so as not to spook him. Picking the fly off the water, I cast a few more times and then let the beetle drop, with a slight curve to the left in the leader, a foot or more in front of the trout. It hit the water rather gently, but evidently some of the naturals don't make a very big splash when they fall from the trees. It no sooner hit the water than the trout darted forward, opened his jaws, gulped the beetle, and headed back to the cover of the wall.

It took me quite by surprise, but I was still able to move the rod tip far enough to the right to take up the slack in the line and set the hook. Fortunately, the trout headed for midstream instead of upstream, where he would have spooked the two trout feeding in front of him. I played him for a minute or two and released an eleven-inch rainbow. The beetle was just in the side of his jaw, a well-taken fly.

Waiting a few minutes until the water calmed down in front of me, I watched for the remaining two trout to rise. Four feet in front of the position the first trout took and just a little to the left, the second trout resumed feeding. I cast the beetle two feet in front of him and it hit the water with very little disturbance. The trout must have been close enough, for as soon as it hit the water he darted forward, settled a few inches beneath the surface, and watched as it floated toward him. Up he came, hesitated for a few seconds, then gently inhaled the imitation beetle. He turned out to be a thirteen-inch brown. *Not bad,* I thought to myself. *Two trout cast to and two trout hooked on the new beetle. Look's like it's going to do all right.*

Working through that stretch of water I hooked and released six more trout and spooked that many also. For those of you who don't know that water, it is very flat, calm, and clear. If your casting is not perfect you can spook more trout than you will ever catch on it. Nevertheless, if you can pinpoint the distance of your feeding trout and cast the fly and line so that it straightens out about three feet above the water, turns over, and drifts down naturally without making any big splash, the chances of taking trout on the surface are very good.

One of the things to remember when you are fishing the kind of water that is very quiet, very calm, and very flat, is to cast a curve to the right or left. As you work a trout, let's say to your right going upstream, you must cast a right curve so that the fly lands in front of your quarry and the leader and line stay to his left, out of his window. If the leader or line comes too close to the trout, he will see the shadow and go down. Even the slightest disturbance in his window will put him down. This is not always the end of the game, however. If you put him down and are willing to stand there and wait for him, he will come back up. Usually five to fifteen minutes is plenty of time. An adept casting technique cannot be stressed enough on this type of water.

One of the nice things about fishing this particular stretch of water was that you didn't have much current or drag with which to contend. Granted, you had perfectly still, calm water that offered no cover whatsoever to the fly and leader as it landed, but you didn't have the problem you had on a stream like the Letort or on a fast piece of broken water. Occasionally it was an advantage and occasionally a disadvantage.

As the summer wears on and you get into late June, July, August, and even early September, depending on where you are fishing you can normally fish beetles anytime during the day and take trout. I'm convinced now, though we weren't sure of it then, that the trout watch for these landbred insects to fall on the water. They may not occur in the numbers that the mayflies do when a hatch is in progress, but I'm certain that all during the day and all summer long, if enough of these terrestrials fall on or get into the water, one way or another the trout will always be on the lookout for them. They will take the beetles without hesitation, and terrestrials are a large part of the trout's normal diet.

There was another spot in this quiet water, just upstream into the woods, that held an unusual number of trout. The trout always seemed to be up and surface feeding. It didn't matter whether you were down there in the early morning, the late morning, or the afternoon. The trout just fed and fed and fed. It was an area that was impossible to approach from the stream because the water was over chest waders. The only way to get to these trout was from the bank. A few of us cleared one or two casting lanes in the brush in order to enable us to get to those trout.

One Sunday morning I went down, walked into the woods, sat in one of the cleared areas, and just watched. There were nineteen trout feeding in an area not more than forty feet long and thirty feet wide. They were feeding consistently, and by that I mean two rises every minute for each of them. I tied on a beetle and tried to cast. I was in the trees and brush more than on the water. "The only way you are going to get a fly to these crazy trout is to roll-cast," I thought to myself as I untangled my leader after the last encounter with the brush. The problem with that solution was that if I cast over any of the trout, they were bound to spook when the line hit the water or when it was being retrieved in readiness for the next roll cast. Things didn't look very encouraging. The only answer seemed to be to start casting to the trout closest to me and then work my way to midstream. My first attempt at these trout was most discouraging, to put it mildly.

One interesting and worthwhile observation did come to light as a result of that first episode, however. When you spooked a trout on the Letort, he would not come back for a good long time. Here, if you spooked these trout either with the roll or pick-up, they would go down for a few minutes and resume feeding almost immediately. The only conclusion I could draw at the time to explain the trout returning to feed that soon was that perhaps they felt more secure under the protection of the overhanging trees.

The black beetle worked very well under the trees. I used sizes #14 and #16. After a time however, these trout became wise just as the Letort trout did and seemed to be able to recognize that imitation beetle. They wouldn't take anything. They would come up and look, drift along under the fly, and always refuse it. Even finer tippets didn't help.

Wondering if the trout really did recognize that pattern, I tied up some brown, yellow, and green deer-hair beetles. Occasionally, a trout could be taken on one of the other colors, but not as easily or as readily as they had originally taken the black beetle. To say the least, it became very frustrating working these surface feeders from the bank.

Not knowing what to do, I felt that a pattern in a smaller size might work. I had watched the water often enough and had used the insect net enough that I knew there were some very small beetles: for instance, the ladybug. How they got there I didn't know, but they showed up in the collection net. There were other types of beetles minute in comparison to the Japanese beetle.

Wondering if perhaps these smaller sizes were the answer, I tied some on #18 hooks, with the clipped deer hair in colors of black, brown, yellow, and green. These had to be fished on 7X tippets. The procedure was the same. Roll-cast and start with the trout nearest the bank and work out toward midstream.

My first attempt with the tiny beetles was quite satisfying. I started fishing to a trout not four feet from the bank and just barely rolled the leader on the water. The tiny beetle hit and the trout dashed to the spot, inhaled the fly, and headed for the bottom. It was a twelve-inch rainbow.

This was an interesting kind of fishing. When these trout fed they lay just a few inches under the surface film. On a day when the water was clear, the light right, and you were using Polaroids, you could see every one of these fish just below the surface. I rolled the fly to the second trout and it landed about three feet in front of him. No way could he have seen it. I let it drift slowly down in the quiet water and as soon as it came into his window he came over, drifted back just a few inches, and took the tiny fooler. The sequence repeated itself for the next five trout that lay out toward midstream. They all took the little black beetle without hesitation. I was pretty sure that it was the size that had made the difference between refusal and acceptance. With the smaller size the trout were once again eager to take the imitation.

What about the other colors? I wondered as I changed flies. In the course of three or four hours I fished the black, brown, yellow, and green, and all of them worked. This was interesting because when I had tried the various colors in the larger size, the trout refused more often then they took. Down in the smaller size, the #18, they took more often than they refused. The only conclusion I could draw at that time was that they would take the big beetle for the Japanese beetle. There must have been a lot of other things falling from those limbs, leaves, and bushes that had the same silhouette and rode in the surface film the same as did the beetle but were much smaller and varied in color. The little imitations are as good as the larger version. We no longer call them Japanese Beetles, but the little Deer-Hair or Clipped Beetle. They worked way back then and are just as effective today, whether on the Breeches, Letort, or any freestone water.

When the terrestrials were being developed and written about I think anglers assumed that the only place they could be used were on limestone waters or meadow streams. This is not the case. The landbred insects get on or in all water. Don't hesitate to fish them on your favorite freestoner.

The Deer-Hair Beetle became quite a productive fly on the Breeches, and over the years that particular pattern has continued to produce when it would be difficult to take trout on other flies. One time in particular comes to mind. A gentleman known to most eastern Pennsylvanians was Harry Alaman, who had a local TV show on Channel 8 in Lancaster, Pennsylvania, called "Call of the Outdoors." Harry once did a film for the Yellow Breeches Anglers. He had been up to film the trout-stocking and nursery operation on the Yellow Breeches. One afternoon he had some time and wanted to get some fishing shots along the stream. I went along and we fished some of the lower water. As we sat having lunch I asked if he would be interested in seeing some of the surface feeders that work in the quiet water all day, every day. He was very receptive to the idea and we headed upstream into the woods. We sat and watched a few of the trout feed in different locations along the bank. There were trout in one particular spot that were always up and feeding. We had cleared a casting lane behind it up along the bank. Harry said he would like to try to set his camera up on the bank and, if possible, get pictures of my casting to the trout, the fly on the water, the trout lying in their feeding positions, coming up, looking, and, we hoped, taking the fly. He had never been able to get a sequence like that because stream or water conditions had never been right.

He found that when he got back up on the bank about fifteen feet behind me and looked through the camera, he could see the trout lying close to the surface in their feeding positions. He could see them come up and feed from the surface. Harry proceeded to get set up and I sat and watched the feeding trout.

When he was ready, I tied on a #14 clipped-deer-hair beetle and began to work on the trout closest to shore. I had to make a dozen or more casts, but all the while I was casting Harry was able to film the fly landing and drifting down to the trout, the trout coming up and inspecting the fly, then going down and refusing the imitation. I'm sorry to say most of the early casts were not taken. I didn't want to put the smaller beetle on because it would not show up on the film. Instead of changing flies, I tied on a piece of extra-fine tippet material, one-half-pound test, I recall. I still was not sure the trout would take and they had seen the size #14 come over them so many times that they were beginning to act finicky. It seemed that they would come look at every cast but then refuse it.

Anyhow, I made a cast with the fine tippet. It landed a couple feet in front of the trout. Harry said, "I've got it. I can see the fly and the trout." As the fly approached the trout's window, the fish came over and under the fly. His nose couldn't have been more than an inch beneath it. He drifted back with the floating imitation and gently sucked it from the surface film. I struck, set the hook, and happily was able to play and land the trout. Harry had his sequence on film. He was excited and happy with the situation and he kept repeating "Boy, I've never seen that; I've never been able to get a shot like that. Everything worked out just great."

Another trip comes to mind that might give freestone fishermen some encouragement to use the terrestrials. Barry Beck, who lives about ninety miles east and north of Carlisle, Pennsylvania, belonged to a local club that leased a piece of water on Big Fishing Creek. They spent a lot of time, money, and manpower on stream improvement, dam construction, and holding water. They bought trout and stocked the water. They initiated no-kill rules for the first several years to give the trout the protection they needed to hold over and reproduce. It was a typical freestone stream: very cold, very fast, and surprisingly full of insect life.

I met Barry at his fly shop where we chatted a bit then drove to the stream. We parked, readied our tackle, and headed to the water as he advised me on where to fish, what to use, and how to approach the water. Barry headed upstream and I fished in front of the car for a while. After about half an hour I decided to head upstream and see how he was doing because I wasn't having all that much luck. I met him upstream where he was working just below a large dam his angling club had put in. The dam backed water up for several hundred yards, was about waist deep, and both sides were lined with brush. He told me there were quite a few trout in the pool, but that they were very tough and spooked rather easily. "Go ahead," I said, "you fish it and I'll watch and take a few lessons."

We stood at the dam breast and watched upstream for trout to rise. There were three or four trout feeding. Barry moved into position to work on them. "What are you going to use?" I questioned. "Probably a cricket or beetle," he returned, going through his fly box. I don't know whether he didn't have any crickets or whether he chose the beetle by chance. Whatever, he tied on a beetle and began to work the rising trout. He rose all four and hooked and landed three of them, which was quite a feat. I hadn't seen any beetles along the brush, but he assured me they did have them and that the beetle really worked, even though that stream didn't have the huge quantities of beetles that we found along the Letort or Breeches. This led me to assume that the trout take the clipped-deer-hair beetle for the Japanese beetle as well as for other insects that find their way into the water. Barry told me that in that particular stretch under the overhanging brush of the quiet water he could almost always count on rising and taking a few trout on that pattern. That was some twenty years or more ago, and though I haven't had the opportunity to fish with him on that water recently, I'm sure he still uses the beetle with just as much success.

The Grass Beetle

Hook: #16 or #18 (Mustad
94840, Tiemco 101)

Thread: 6/0 Fly Master
Brown

Hackle: Brown

Overwing: Natural raffia
grass, dyed brown

1. Insert hook in vise. Attach tying thread in the center of the hook shank.
2. Tie in a 1/8-inch strip of raffia grass and wind back to rear of hook shank.
3. Select proper size hackle and tie in at rear of hook shank.
4. Palmer hackle tightly forward to within 1/8 inch of hook eye. Tie off. Half-hitch.
5. Clip a "V" on top and bottom of hook shank.
6. Pull the strip of raffia over the top of the hackle and tie off at hook eye.
7. Using a dubbing needle, at the hook rear fold the raffia grass over the needle. This will produce a wide, yet flat, fold at the hook bend, and will improve the silhouette of the fly.
8. Build an enlarged head. Whip-finish. Apply head cement to the fly head and coat the top of the raffia grass overwing with clear lacquer.

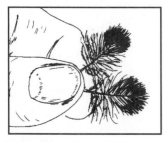

1. Select two green feathers from a ring-necked pheasant head.

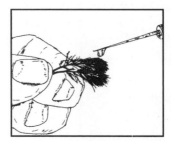

2. Apply head cement to one side of each feather..

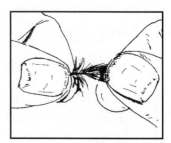

3. Press together the sides of the feathers that are wet with the head cement.

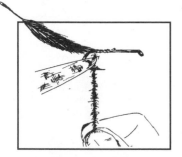

7. Dub a small amount of black fur on thread.

8. Wrap the dubbed thread forward to a point just behind the hook eye.

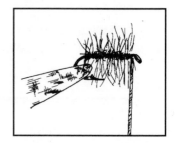

9. Palmer the hackle to the front of the hook. Tie off.

The Japanese Beetle

Hook: #14 or #16 (Mustad 94840, Tiemco 100)

Thread: Black

Body: Black dubbed fur

Hackle: Black

Wing: Green ring-necked pheasant feathers

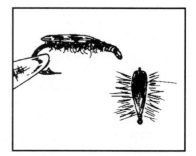

13. The fly is complete.

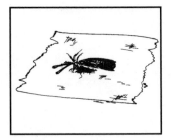

4. Place the feathers on a piece of waxed paper to dry.

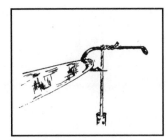

5. Insert hook in vise and attach thread directly above the hook point.

6. Tie in black hackle at rear of hook.

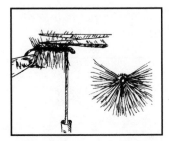

10. Clip a "V" in top of the hackle.

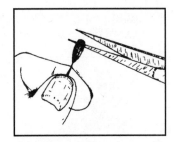

11. Clip the pheasant-feather wing so that it is rounded on the back end.

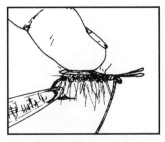

12. Tie the pheasant-feather wing flat on top of the hook shank. Whip-finish the head of the fly.

1. Insert hook in vise and attach thread directly above the hook point.
2. Wrap thread from back to front along the shank. Half-hitch.
3. Tie on the the preshaped foam rubber wing.
4. Tie in black hackle.
5. Wrap two turns of hackle and tie off.
6. Clip off excess hackle.
7. Whip-finish head.
8. Clip a "V" on top and bottom of hackle. The fly is complete.

The Foam-Rubber Beetle

Hook: #14, #16, #18 (Mustad 94840, Tiemco 100)

Thread: Black

Hackle: Black for legs

Wing: Black foam rubber trimmed to an oval beetle shape

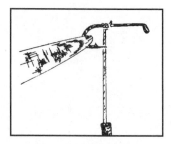

1. Insert hook in vise and attach thread directly above the hook point.

2. Clip a small bunch of dyed-black deer hair (the bunch should be about the thickness of a lead pencil for a size #14, and proportionately less for #16 or #18).

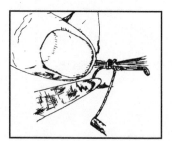

3. Holding the deer hair between thumb and forefinger, lay it on top of the hook shank. Make two loose turns with the thread in the middle of the bunch.

7. Repeat steps 2 through 6 until the hook shank is completely packed with flared deer hair. Whip-finish head.

8. Clip the deer hair flat on top of the beetle.

9. Clip the deer hair flat on the bottom of the beetle.

Deer-Hair Beetle

Hook: #14, #16, #18 (Mustad 94840, Tiemco 100)

Thread: Black

Body: Black deer hair

  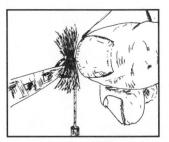

4. Pull the thread tight. The hair will flare up in front of and behind the thread.

5. Wrap the thread forward, through the deer hair, to the edge of the bunch of hair. Half-hitch just in front of the bunch.

6. With the thumb and forefinger of the right hand, push the flared bunch of hair toward rear of hook shank and pack it tight.

10. Clip the deer hair into an oval shape on both sides of the beetle. The fly is complete.

The Willow Beetle

Hook: #18 or #24 (Mustad 94840, Tiemco 100)

Thread: Black, brown, green, or yellow

Body: Black, brown, green, or yellow deer hair

Follow the tying instructions for the Deer-Hair Beetle. The only differences between that fly and the Willow Beetle are hook size, thread, and body color.

Ants

If I were to make a selection of the most productive and consistent trout-taking patterns of the terrestrials, I suppose it would have to be the ants. All round, I don't think they can be beat.

Ant patterns have been around for a long time. In *Fishing the Midge* I wrote of the Wet Ant or the Hard-back Ant. I'm not sure how long ago they were originated, but I do know they have been around for a lot longer than I've been fishing. I'm not certain those early patterns were the result of testing, as the floating ant patterns were when they were developed on the Letort. The difference with these is that they are dry ants that float in the surface film just as the rest of the terrestrial patterns do. They have dubbed fur bodies with hackle in the middle or at the head of the fly. They are tied on lightwire hooks instead of the old heavy wet-fly hooks used for the sinking ants.

With the increased knowledge and experience the locals gained in taking trout on terrestrials, it became evident that the ants played just as important a part in the trout's diet as did the Jassids and beetles. Checking the water on the Letort or the Yellow Breeches with an insect net, we found that for every leafhopper or beetle, there were probably two or three ants. The trout could feed on ants two or three times as often as they could on the leafhoppers or beetles.

I don't know how or why the ants get on the water. A bird landing on the limb of a tree or in the edge of the grass would be enough disturbance to dislodge and knock the ants into the water. Gusty winds inevitably blow them in. These are things to remember whenever or wherever you happen to be fishing.

I'm not sure there is any way for the fly rodder to determine when the trout are feeding on ants. But if you have an occasion to be on the stream and are getting more refusals than strikes, an ant pattern may change your luck.

Our first ants were tied with fur bodies. Some tiers used seal fur, others black rabbit hair, still others spun fur or angora hair. (Today the preblended fur is much easier to dub and preblended fur in the right colors is even better.) Two humps were tied on the front and back halves of the hook shank, with a hackle wound in the middle. It may not have been the perfect imitation of an ant, but it sure did work. Some local tiers went even further and tied a three-humped ant: a hump at the rear, a second hump in the middle (a little smaller than the first), and a third small hump at the head. The hackle was tied between the first and second segments or the second and third segments, depending on the tier's preference. Either way worked.

The advent of the floating ant produced trout for us better than any of the previous patterns. We originally tied them in sizes #16, #18, and #20. Later, we went down to #22 and #24, and eventually to #26 and #28 as the hooks became available. Size #18 was the most popular size. If you started fishing any stretch of stream with the #18 black ant you could count on taking at least a few trout. If you happened to run into a particularly tough or selective feeder, he could nearly always be fooled by a smaller size. A lighter tippet than was normally used for the #18 was necessary: 7X or 8X worked well with a #22 or #24 ant.

The original ant patterns were just black. Stands to reason, because any ants that I'd ever paid any attention to were black. But that simple approach to color was just another lesson waiting to be learned.

Not all ants are black. Not a very brilliant deduction you might say, but how many of us overlook the most obvious and simple realities every time we fish a favorite stretch of water? I don't know who can be credited with tying the first brown or cinnamon ant, but one thing is sure, he was an observant, progressive, and learned angler. Ed Shenk showed me my first fur ants.

The cinnamon ants proved to be even more effective than the black pattern at the right time and in the right place. The pattern was tied with a brown-colored fur that can best be described as cinnamon. Shake some cinnamon from a spice can on a piece of white paper and try to duplicate the color in the fur you use. The only place I was able to find this fur was from a supply house in New York. It proved (for me, Ed Shenk, and others) to be the most effective color for the brown or cinnamon ant. The cinnamon ant was tied just like the black ant: a hump in the back, brown hackle in the middle, and a hump in the front, size #18 to #24.

How logical or illogical are we anglers? This brings to mind an interesting story. To set the background, the reader must understand what was happening on the limestone water in the Cumberland Valley in the early days of terrestrial experimentation. A new plateau had been reached in fly-fishing techniques, theory, and tying. It was challenging and exciting; it had everyone involved in observing and experimenting.

We had a retired army captain who really got involved. His name was Chuck Kissinger. He has since passed on. Like the rest of us, he was happy when things were going well. When they weren't, he would get down in the dumps for days at a time. I've never known anyone to get as frustrated as he did.

One day he came into my shop, the Yellow Breeches Angler, wearing a grin as big as a watermelon; we didn't say a word, even though Ed Shenk and I knew darn well something was up. After a few customers had come and gone and almost an hour had passed, Chuck couldn't stand it any longer.

"Hey, you guys," he started, "if I show you something, will you promise not to make fun?" "Sure," we agreed. "What do you have now?"

"If you guys laugh," he started, pacing back and forth in front of the fly-tying bench, "I'll never show you another thing."

Shenk looked at me, I looked at him, and we both thought he must really have found something. "All right," we promised. He had us quite curious by this time.

Bending over the tying bench, he dumped a plastic box of flies in front of us, three dozen or so in varying sizes. "Ants," Shenk muttered, evidently disappointed not to be seeing some new secret on the bench. "They look real good," he said.

"Aw, look at them, you dummies," Chuck fired back. We began to spread the pile of ants on the bench. There in the middle of the pile were Chuck's new secret: a half dozen "white" ants in three or four sizes.

"Holy cow! White ants. What are they for?" I blurted. Shenk just looked. "Are you pulling our legs or do you plan on having some fun with the visitors?" I queried.

"Okay, make fun, only don't ask me for any when we're on the Letort and you find they work," he shot back as he picked up his new creations.

"Come on, you can't be serious," Shenk came back with a half-believing tone in his voice.

"Alright, never mind," said Chuck. And off he went to the Letort.

Shenk and I really had some fun after he left, discussing the possibilities of white ants. Neither of us were really sure of what he had. He gave us something with which to pass the afternoon and by suppertime Chuck was back. "How'd you do?" Shenk asked as Chuck got a soda and sat down.

"Not bad, not bad," he replied. He gave no details whatsoever on the afternoon's fishing or the white ants.

"Did you try them?" I asked.

"What?" as he took a long deliberate slug of soda.

"The white ants," Shenk chimed in.

"Oh, them. Yeah," he said.

"Well?" from both Shenk and me.

"Caught a couple," and that ended Chuck's conversation about the new ants.

We'd really done it. We put him down without giving him a fair chance to tell us the whys and wherefores. He knew he had something and wasn't about to let us in on it. For days we both wondered about it. Did they really work or was he waiting for us to tie some and show him so he could laugh himself silly? This was known to happen among the Letort regulars now and again.

Ed and I both tied some white ants, half afraid not to.

They worked! Don't ask me why. To this day I've never seen a live white ant. Want some advice? They'll make a good conversation piece and someday they'll catch you a trout. When I tied the flies for Norm Shires to take pictures of for a slide show we do, I included the white ant. It makes for a good story, whether the audience takes it seriously or not.

The point is this: *something* looks like that white ant to the trout, because they *will* take them.

One of the points made in every fly-fishing book is that the reader should learn what flies are on the water he fishes regularly. The same point will be made in this book. Not only mayflies, caddisflies, and midges, but learn also what terrestrials are on your water. Whether it's a freestone or a limestone stream, the more you know about the water and the insect life in and around it, the better off you are going to be and the more trout you are going to take.

If, in observing your water, you come across the flying ant hatch you are in for some of the most fantastic fishing you will ever experience. I'm not sure when these hatches occur on different streams. I know that here in the Cumberland Valley it can be as early as June and as late as August or September. When the flying ants come out or hatch or whatever you want to call it, the trout go wild. They will feed for as long as the ants keep coming to the water. I've seen these feeding sprees both here and in the West.

If you don't get enough time on your water to determine when these occurrences take place, find yourself a fishing partner from a local club or organization who gets to spend more time astream than you do. Chances are, he'll know what's going on. When you attend local club meetings or clinics, ask questions about the water.

The flying ants I've seen are brown in color, perhaps a little darker than the color we use for the cinnamon ants. However, once the fur gets a little wet it matches the color of the flying ants closely enough to make it effective.

There are stretches of water on the Letort that get fantastic numbers of flying ants. The perfect situation is when the wind begins to blow. The helpless little ants are blown on the water in unbelievable numbers and the trout feed in a frenzy.

Broken tippets and lost flies are a common complaint of first-timers. During the flying ant hatch the trout seem to abandon all fear or caution. You can make bad casts and not put them down for long. You can get closer to the trout than you normally could. You may even prick a trout or two and they will come back to the very next cast, even though you know they felt the sting of the barb.

On the Breeches where wading is permitted, you can get to within several feet of the trout when the ants are on the water. If you do happen to put one down, nine times out of ten he will resume feeding within a matter of minutes.

Another nice thing about the ant flights is that you do not have to cast a long line. A ten- or twelve-foot leader and maybe ten feet of line is more than enough for this type of fishing.

The flying ants are generally small. I've heard anglers see them as large as a #12 or #14, but on our water a #20 or #22 is the most common size.

If you tie the cinnamon ants, tie a few with blue dun hackles instead of the brown. The wing of the flying ant is definitely a dun gray in color. The dun-hackled ant works better for the flying ant imitation than does the brown hackled pattern. Some tiers will tie hackle-tip wings flat over the body of the ant. This type of tie will work even better than the standard hackle tie.

I'll never forget my first encounter with the flying ants on the Yellow Breeches. I was fishing the lower section in the fast water with terrestrials. It was late morning, and suddenly the air was filled with flying ants. The water began to boil with trout. It was easy to determine what to use. I tied on a size #20 cinnamon ant, dressed it with silicone, and began to work on the trout rising around me. In an area of about forty feet there had to be a dozen trout gorging themselves on the tiny ants. When I cast to the first trout, not ten feet from me, the fly just hit the water when he jumped on it as though he hadn't eaten in days. In a matter of minutes the tiny 6 1/2-foot rod guided a twelve-inch brown to the net. I squeezed the fly on my shirt sleeve to dry it and cast to trout number two. The fly landed just a few inches to his left. He turned, came to the fly, and inhaled it without any hesitation. He was a ten-inch rainbow. Without taking a step, I caught and released two more trout. I still had not cast more than fifteen feet.

The ants were on the water for forty-five minutes or more. In that length of time I hooked and released seventeen trout. I snapped off more flies than I care to remember, and missed many risers.

More years ago than I care to remember I took a vacation to Vermont. My main reason for going was to visit with Tony Skilton, who at that time was working at the Orvis Company during the summer while attending college back in Pennsylvania. The second reason was that it would give me an opportunity to fish with Tony on water with which he had become very familiar. We wanted to fish the terrestrials on the famed Battenkill to see if they would produce as well as they did on our limestoners back home. We could fish mornings and evenings. During the middle of the day, I figured that the family and I could get in some sightseeing and

Terrestrial Fishing

even do a little antiquing. It was a great way to do things the family enjoyed and still get in some fishing.

Tony, of course, was no stranger to the terrestrial patterns. He grew up in Boiling Springs, Pennsylvania, and had learned his trouting on the Yellow Breeches, Letort, Green Spring, and Big Spring. By the time he was a junior in high school he had become an accomplished fly fisherman and fly tier. Attending college in the north-central part of the state, he had the opportunity to apply his limestone tactics on some of the best freestone waters of Pennsylvania.

Tony took me to a stretch of the river along Route 7, south of Manchester. We parked at a bridge and walked upstream. The section he had selected was long, flat, and very quiet. Alder bushes were thick on both banks, necessitating wading. We waded into the tail end of the quiet water. It was surprisingly deep, almost to the top of our waders. We stood and watched for a long time, trying to pick out the telltale ring or dimple of a feeding trout along the brush. There were a few sporadic rises, though not nearly as many as we'd hoped to find. The closest was fifty feet or so upstream.

"You take the first one," I said, moving to Tony's left and giving him casting room. "I'll try to see what happens."

False-casting, he edged forward almost ten feet in order to give himself better control of the cast. His line shot through the air, the leader turned over perfectly, and the fly landed about three feet in front of the trout. Slowly, ever so slowly, it drifted toward the spot where the trout had risen. Nothing. It was a perfect cast and float.

"Do you think I spooked him?" asked Tony.

"I doubt it. Try again. This time drop the fly a foot or so downstream, closer to where he rose," I replied.

His second cast was also perfect, landing just barely a foot in front of where we had seen the ring. The leader was curved away from the fly's line of drift.

"He's got to take that one," I whispered. The tiny ant drifted once more over the spot where we had seen the ring in the water. Nothing.

"Something's wrong. He should have jumped all over that," I told Tony consolingly.

Tony mended line and picked the fly from the water. He checked the leader for knots and examined the fly. "Nothing wrong here. Maybe I should try a different pattern."

"No, not yet," I answered. "Try him once more, only this time get the fly in closer to the bank. Get it about a foot or so to the left of where we saw his rise."

For the third time Tony made a flawless cast. The fly hit just above where the trout had come up. It hadn't drifted six inches when a tiny dimple broke the surface. Before I could yell "strike," Tony's rod tip came up, pulling the leader and line off the water. The hook bit home and the trout headed for the protection of the brush. Carefully, Tony played him in and under the brush. In a few minutes he led a twelve-inch brown to net. "Nice work," I congratulated.

"Thanks. He had me wondering there for a while," Tony replied.

"I think he was lying back under the brush a little farther than we thought, and coming out in the current a little as food drifted by."

"Probably," he answered, drying the fly.

We both watched upstream for more trout. "There's one," Tony said, pointing midstream. "Try him." He moved to his left while I edged out toward midstream. I worked out line and sent the tiny ant through the air.

"A little behind him," Tony commented.

I picked the fly from the water, stripped out line, and let it go again. This time it landed too far to the trout's right. "He's not going to see it," Tony whispered. The third cast was better, landing just a few inches to the left of where we had seen the rise. "He got it!" Tony shouted, even before I could see the ring begin to break the surface film. Quickly, I raised the rod tip and could feel the hook bite home. The trout dug for the bottom, holding his own for a little while against the light tippet and tiny hook. Before long another brown, smaller than the first, was released.

"Not bad," Tony commented. "Two tries, two trout on the ants."

Taking turns, we must have released another half dozen before fishing our way out of the tangle of brush and quiet water.

"That was fun," I remarked, climbing onto the bank. "They weren't as easy as I thought they would be."

"No, that's why I brought you down here," he replied, sitting down next to me. "I've fished this a number of times this summer and found the trout in this particular stretch to be some of the toughest on the river. It's pretty good when there's a hatch in progress, but during the day when you only see the occasional riser, they've been very frustrating. Really, we did better than I thought we would."

Walking back to the bridge we both felt a little better about what had just transpired.

Another interesting ant incident occurred in 1974. I went to West Yellowstone, Montana, to attend a Federation of Fly Fishers meeting, do some demonstration fly-tying, and sit in on a panel discussion. It was the week before Labor Day. I was not scheduled for anything on Sunday, and on the advice of Bud Lilly I decided to drive to Idaho, about forty minutes away, and fish the Trico hatch on The Henry's Fork of the Snake River at Railroad Ranch.

I got up early and drove over to Will Godfrey's shop in Last Chance, right on the river. He wasn't open, so I walked next door to a small restaurant and had some breakfast. After I'd downed about four cups of coffee, some fishermen drove up to Will's shop and found it open. I hurried over, got a license, and asked the young lad working there where I should go. "Don't matter," he said. "Once the flies start there will be fish all over the river." Great, I thought to myself, stuffing my license into my wallet and heading for the door. I drove to the bridge at the lower end of the ranch and expected it to be mobbed. I could not believe what I saw—there wasn't a fisherman in sight! Had this been Pennsylvania, there would have been fishermen up and down the river as far as one could see. Bewildered and wondering whether I had really found The Henry's Fork, I got out of the rental car and walked to the river's edge. I couldn't believe my eyes! The river was twenty to thirty times as wide as the Letort and appeared to be ten feet deep. To add to the surprise of the river and the dilemma that I apparently faced, there were Tricos in the air and on the water as far as I could see. Trout were sipping and gulping everywhere. I finally managed to gain my composure and began to fish. For more than two hours I experienced some of the most fantastic trout fishing of my life.

When things began to slow down, I waded to the river's edge and sat down to reflect on the morning's experience. Suddenly the water's surface began to boil with rising trout. Swarms of flies were everywhere. Puzzled, I waded back into the river. For fifteen minutes or more I cast again and again to the rising trout without a single rise to my Trico. The clouds of flies were thick in the air, but I could not tell what the trout were taking. One thing was sure—it wasn't Tricos.

I pulled out my small pocket seine and held it in the water for ten seconds or so. The net was covered with tiny flying ants—cinnamon, not black. I could have fished for hours with my Trico imitation and never touched a fish.

I quickly tied a size #22 cinnamon ant to the 7X tippet and in a matter of minutes hooked and released the first three trout I cast to. I relaxed a little to observe the feeding trout. There must have been thousands of ants on the water; the trout's feeding activity was frenzied compared to their Trico taking. I then fooled four more trout without moving.

Forty yards upstream a pod of four or five trout were working. One was definitely a good trout. As he rose his entire head almost came out of the water, as though he were trying to inhale a dozen ants with each gulp. The head was broad, at least by eastern standards. When the head went down the dorsal fin broke the water, and then I was certain it was a "good" trout. Before moving I changed ants, having caught seven on the one I was using, and tied on a new tippet just to be sure.

Slowly, I worked upriver to within sixty feet of the feeding trout and made several false casts to be sure of the distance. I let the line go, turning it over high above the water and allowing the line and leader to straighten out completely so the tiny ant would land on the surface without making a dimple. The fly hadn't drifted six inches when the surface broke and the rod tip rose reflexively. I felt the weight of the trout as he took off for the protection of the weeds. Don't think it's the big one, I told myself as I stripped in line with rod held high to keep pressure on the churning trout. A few minutes later a heavy-bodied fourteen-inch rainbow come to net. "That's not him," I whispered as I returned the trout to the water.

The three remaining trout continued to feed as though nothing had happened. Drying the fly and dressing it with silicone, I slowly waded another ten feet closer to the rising trout. Casting again, I dropped the tiny ant about two feet in front of the feeding trio. The instant the fly touched the water I quickly lowered the rod parallel to the surface, allowing enough line slack to keep the ant from dragging. This time, the fly drifted about a foot before another dimple appeared in the surface film. I struck and instantly the trout headed for the middle of the Snake. He was heavy, and line peeled from the reel with that beautiful singing sound. The rod was bent almost in half from the weight of the heavy trout and the pressure of the current as the fish bore into the weeds in midstream. The backing knot went through the stripping guide. I eased up a little on the rod pressure and the trout held, shaking violently. I felt the strong throbbing of his shaking carry well down into the rod butt. "That's him," I almost shouted out loud as though there was someone with me. "The big one." For almost ten minutes the weight and strength of the trout kept him in control, and then gradually I reeled in line, turning the trout from the middle of the river. He wasn't done in yet, so I began to give line. More minutes passed and I finally got a glimpse of him. He was heavy and appeared to be at least eighteen inches long. I worked my way slowly toward the river bank, wanting to be able to measure this one and get a picture. In another few minutes he slid into the net.

I laid the rod in the grass so the trout could be placed along the handle and butt section where a thread wrap at twenty inches marked the rod. He was tired now and seemed to appreciate the chance to rest. After lifting him from the water and placing him along the rod in the grass, I saw he was an inch-and-a-half past the twenty-inch mark—a heavy, deep-bodied, brilliantly colored rainbow. I snapped two quick pictures and returned him to the water at the edge of the bank. He lay there finning, spent from the twenty-minute ordeal. For the longest while I watched him to be sure he was okay. I thought to myself, "An eastern angler might fish a lifetime back home and never see a trout this size." Fortunately, I was able to find, hook, and release one on my first experience on this fabled river. Western anglers are fortunate indeed! Eventually the trout's strength returned, he swam upstream and then turned and headed for the middle of the Snake and safety.

The ants were on the water that day for about an hour-and-a-half. They vanished just as quickly as they appeared. I hooked and released eleven trout on the tiny cinnamon imitations. As I walked back to the car, the vastness, beauty, tranquility, and trout of The Henry's Fork were etched in my memory, and I have recalled them again and again on cold snowy winter nights ever since. I couldn't wait to get back to West Yellowstone and relate my experience to Bud Lilly.

My close friend and regular angling companion, Norm Shires, is an ardent wet-fly fisherman. He was brought up on wet-fly fishing as a youngster in the Pocono streams of Pennsylvania. He fishes only three patterns, which I am not at liberty to divulge, and catches and releases more trout in a season than many anglers do in a lifetime. His brother, Rich, who did the black-and-white tying illustrations for the second edition of my midge book (as well as for this one), is equally as adept with *his* three wet flies. Norm loves dry-fly fishing, but during the early half of the season, when a hatch is not in progress, he can drum up more than enough trout with his wets. From midsummer through fall, though, his favorite is the ant. While I ply the water with crickets, hoppers, beetles, and inchworms, ninety percent of the time Norm's confidence is with the ants. That word, *confidence*, is his secret. He has confidence in the ants and as a result has amazing success on days astream. While I change from one terrestrial pattern to another I take a lot of fish, but more times than not he will take just as many and often more on his ants. There is a lesson to be learned from Norm's confidence factor.

Some years ago Norm and I had a chance to spend a weekend in north-central Pennsylvania on one of our better freestone streams, a three-and-a-half mile regulated area on White Deer Creek. We arrived at the campground on Friday and spent the evening on Fishing Creek above the hatchery at Lamar, another regulated stretch of blue ribbon trout water.

The following morning we decided not to cook breakfast in camp and drove to a truck stop just off Interstate 81. We had a big leisurely breakfast, knowing it would be a long time before lunch. After several cups of coffee and a lot of talk about the morning's strategy, we drove over the mountain to the fly area. Parking somewhere in the upper half of the area, we hiked one of the many trails down into the valley. This was Norm's first trip to this stream. I had fished it regularly years ago and hadn't been there in a long time until the summer before. My first trip back was a pleasant surprise. The fly-fishing-only regulations were working well; the entire length of the regulated area held a good population of trout.

Upon reaching the stream, Norm said he would walk downstream. I would work upstream. We rigged up over small talk and went our separate ways. It was a beautiful morning, cool for July, which would make for comfortable fishing for three or four hours.

I started with a Letort Hopper, size #16, and in the first hundred yards or so landed four ten- to twelve-inch trout. Then I changed to a Letort Cricket, size #16, and in another quarter-mile of water landed five more fish, two of which were native brook trout of five inches. I still can't figure how a trout that size can even get a cricket that big in its mouth.

Then I came upon a long pool I didn't recognize from prior trips. A huge tree had blown down on the right bank and lay completely across the stream and about thirty feet over the left bank. Branches were still intact and provided good cover. Three trout were feeding behind the tree in the lower end of the pool. One cast, which I felt was pretty good, put them down and sent them scurrying for the protection of the submerged limbs. I reeled in my line, disgusted at myself for spooking the trout.

I walked out around the tree, got on my hands and knees, and inched my way into position to see the upper half of the pool above the blown-down tree. Seven trout were cruising and feeding: the smallest about fourteen inches and the largest around eighteen to twenty inches. The closest trout was only about twenty feet from my position in the grass. Casting sidearm and hoping the movement of the rod wouldn't spook the closest trout, I dropped the cricket to the left of the brown close to the bank. I hoped he would see it hit the water and turn to look. He did just that. He swam over and without hesitation gulped the little cricket. I struck, keeping the rod high and the line tight, hoping to hold or turn him before he could bolt upstream. It worked and I was able to land him well behind the other trout—a nice fourteen-inch brown.

The next trout came to the fly, looked, turned, and went deep. The third trout took and was a twin to number one.

The two largest trout were next in line. On the first cast the closest fish turned, looked at the cricket, and refused. On the second cast there was not even a look, and the third cast put him down. The third trout came to the first cast with the cricket, looked, then turned and followed the fly with his snout just beneath the surface. Suddenly he turned, headed upstream, and disappeared into deep water. I was thoroughly deflated. "Oh, well, I'll try them on my way back," I thought, heading upstream. After fishing another quarter-mile or so I released two more trout. From the time I started, I had either spooked or missed twice as many trout as I had hooked. I looked at my watch and noticed it was past lunch time, so I headed back downstream to meet Norm. As we walked the trail back to the truck we swapped our morning's experiences. He had taken several more trout than I, and guess what he used: black ants.

While eating lunch Norm commented, "Great morning, a really great morning. I found one trout that I'll never forget."

"Watch out," I thought. Norm is sometimes a man of few words and profound and serious a great deal of the time. I didn't know what was coming, but I knew it was going to be worth listening to.

To set the stage for his memorable morning's experience, he described in detail a pool on the stream where his encounter took place. He had come upon the pool, which was about thirty to forty feet wide and seventy or eighty feet long. Across the middle of it a huge tree had fallen over the water. It had been there a long time because all of the branches and limbs were gone and only the trunk remained.

Norm fishes slowly and covers every inch of the water from bank to bank whether fishing upstream with dries or downstream with his wet flies. He is a methodical angler, spending three or four times as long on a good pool or feeding trout as I ever do. He enjoys this approach. It relaxes him and helps him unwind. Not getting astream as often as I or many other anglers, Norm's method is also his therapy. Mastering difficult stream situations and defeating difficult trout becomes his memorable measure of success.

As Norm approached the tail of the pool, he spotted a trout rising fifteen or twenty feet upstream of the log and to the left bank. He worked his way along the left bank into position behind the log, only to find it was impossible to cast because of the tree limbs and brush on the bank above. He backed off and crossed to the right bank to discover the same difficulties. Backing off again and cautiously wading up the middle of the pool, he found that deep water prevented his reaching the log. He had encountered one of perhaps six pools in three miles too deep for hippers.

Watching the trout feed, he contemplated his situation and possible approach. Looking downstream and then upstream, he found he had an open casting lane in the middle of the stream. His only problem was that he would have to cast over the log about twenty feet to reach his quarry. He was ten feet or so behind the log and was looking at a cast of possibly thirty to thirty-five feet with the fly line going over the log. If the trout took, he could only hope the fish would stay in the upper section of the pool long enough to give him time to wade to the right-hand bank, reach the log, and carry on the fight from a vantage point more in his own favor.

Tying on an ant (what else), he went to work. He got in three or four casts that were more than a foot to the trout's right side. The ant floated gingerly past the trout on the tranquil surface of the pool and got not even a look. False-casting several times to develop line speed, Norm drove the rod tip forward fast. Line shot through the air, turning over tightly and then straightening out not more than a foot above the water. His ant landed several feet in front of the trout's station. Slowly, the tiny terrestrial began its journey down the placid pool. As the fly approached, the trout came up and looked, drifted back with the fly, and then, in story-book fashion, opened its jaws, broke the water's surface, and inhaled the tiny imitation. Norm struck and the trout took off upstream, firmly hooked. It shook, dove deep, and shook some more. It was stronger and larger than Norm realized. Holding his rod high and reeling in line, Norm worked his way to the right bank and upstream toward the log. The trout never stopped fighting for a second, but Norm was able to relax a little as he played it. For several minutes he was in control and certain he had won the fight. Suddenly the trout was near the surface, giving Norm his first good look at his adversary. It was larger than he expected, fourteen inches plus, deep-bodied and brightly colored—a good trout for this water. Just as suddenly as it had surfaced it flipped, bore deep into the pool, and headed downstream toward the log. Line peeled from the reel while Norm applied maximum pressure with the rod, hoping the tiny tippet would not break. The tippet held, but the trout made it under the log and into the roots on the far bank. Dropping the rod tip and leaving slack in the line, Norm could only hope the trout would head into the deeper water midstream. It didn't, and Norm felt the line go limp. The trout had won. It had, perhaps, engaged in this same routine many times before with many different anglers and many different imitations. In essence, both were victorious—the trout for its escape and Norm for mastering a difficult situation and outwitting a worthy adversary.

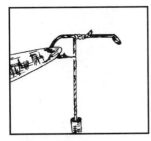

1. Insert hook in vise and attach thread directly above the hook point.

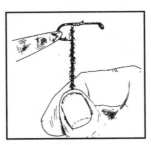

2. Dub a small amount of fur on thread.

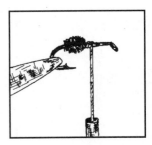

3. Dub a ball of fur on rear half of hook.

4. Tie in hackle. Clip off excess stem.

5. Wrap two or three turns of hackle. Tie off. Clip off excess hackle tip.

6. Dub a ball of fur on front half of hook.

The Fur Body Ant

Hook: #16, #18, #20, #22, #24 (Mustad 94840, Tiemco 101)

Thread: Black, brown, or white

Body: Black, brown (cinnamon), or white

Hackle: Black, ginger, or white

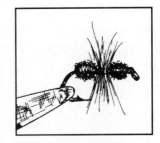

7. Whip-finish head. Apply head cement. The fly is complete.

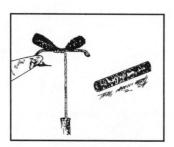

1. Insert hook in vise and attach thread directly above hook point.

2. Tie on oval or flat pre-shaped foam body at center of hook shank.

3. Tie in black hackle.

4. Wrap hackle two or three turns. Tie off and clip excess.

5. Whip-finish head. Apply head cement. The fly is complete.

Rubber Body Ant

Hook: #16 to #24 (Mustad 94840, Tiemco 101)

Thread: Black

Body: Black

Hackle: Black

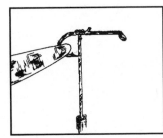

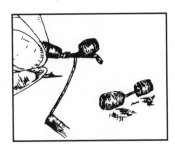

1. Insert hook in vise and attach thread directly above hook point.

2. Tie on prefinished McMurray body.

3. Tie in hackle. Clip off excess stem.

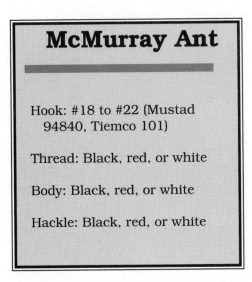

McMurray Ant

Hook: #18 to #22 (Mustad 94840, Tiemco 101)

Thread: Black, red, or white

Body: Black, red, or white

Hackle: Black, red, or white

4. Wrap two turns of hackle. Tie off and clip excess.

5. Apply head cement and the fly is complete.

The Letort Hopper

I grew up in the late 1930s and early 1940s in the hard-coal, or anthracite, region of Pennsylvania. What few streams there were within walking or biking distance of town were devoid of any living creature. One, called Black Creek, was just that: black running water that looked like flowing tar from the coal washeries scattered along its entire length. The other creek had an even neater name, Sulphur Creek, and ran a rust-orange color from the acid-mine drainage. Not much enticement for a young lad to develop an interest in fishing. Fortunately, my parents had close friends who lived in Stillwater, a rural village along Fishing Creek in Montour County. I can remember spending every opening day on Fishing Creek until I left home for college. When I was about twelve my Dad somehow found out about Pennsylvania's famous Fisherman's Paradise on Spring Creek near Bellefonte, not far from State College, Pennsylvania. It was there that my love of fly fishing was born and nurtured for ten consecutive summers.

In those early years, the only hopper imitation I'd ever seen was a pattern tied by Phillips Fly Company of Alexandria, Pennsylvania. There was a lunch stand at Paradise and a huge fly display that must have had 250 or more patterns in it. I stood by the hour over the years looking at those flies and trying to memorize patterns I would try to tie at home. If my memory is correct, the flies cost twenty-five cents, a lot of money for a youngster whose father made about twenty dollars a week in the coal mines.

One of the hoppers in the display had a red tail, yellow wool body, turkey-feather wing tied wet-fly style, and big brown hackle in front. The other had a red tail, yellow deer hair clipped square on top, bottom, and sides, and a turkey-feather and deer-hair wing. It was much too complicated for a young angler of twelve to attempt.

The evolution of the Letort Hopper was no overnight event. For years Charlie Fox, Vince Marinaro, Norm Lightner, Tommy Thomas, Ross Trimmer, Ed Shenk, Carl Norton, and others concocted hopper imitations, the likes of which I had never even dreamed about. As I was sitting on the bench one day with Charlie, he opened his fly box and began picking out hoppers, placing them on the plank between us and relating a story for each one: who tied it, and whether the tier had fished with it on the Letort with Charlie or had sent it to him with a letter. Either way, each presenter extolled the virtues of his particular pattern and the success Charlie could anticipate with the Letort browns.

How sorry I am that in those early days I never had the presence of mind to record the endless hours of conversation with Charlie, the regulars, and the hundreds of visitors to the Letort, for those occasions were the beginning of the legend of that stream. Each and every story was a vital portion of what should have become a part of limestone angling history. Today that history is in the memories of the fly fishers of the Letort.

As Charlie took the next hopper from his fly box he remarked, "This has been my favorite over the years, tied by a good friend of mine from Alexandria." To my amazement, there in the palm of Charlie's hand was the yellow-deer-hair clipped-bodied hopper I had admired so longingly in the display at Paradise fifteen years earlier. It seems Charlie knew Mr. Phillips well and had fished with him regularly for years.

One had to know Vince Marinaro to understand his penchant for perfection. Whether it was tying flies, constructing leaders, building bamboo rods, writing, photography, or studying insects and trout, his ultimate goal was perfection. The result of his fifty-plus years in pursuit of trout has given the angling world some of its most startling discoveries. His classic *A Modern Dry Fly Code* will be required reading for generations of future anglers.

For Vince and Charlie, during the early years the meadows along the Letort were fertile with hoppers. In those days they had the water to themselves, save for a half-dozen or so other regulars who spent many frustrating hours in quest of the elusive native brown trout. Charlie knew every trout, where it lived, when it fed, and what it ate. For several seasons he and Vince had pursued a huge brown, who, when hopper season came, had become a thorn in Vince's side. No matter what fly was presented and no matter how perfectly presented (and if anyone was capable of a perfect presentation, those two were), the hopper-feeding brown eluded them. They had studied his habits for hours, days, and weeks over several seasons: where he lived, his feeding position in the river, how the current carried hoppers to him, the drift of the naturals and their imitations from behind, above, and across stream. They would spend an entire morning observing their adversary, perhaps making only four casts that could be called perfect, but still the trout prevailed.

Vince finally had enough. He went to work on a hopper imitation. This was a challenge he was determined to win. He returned to the stream several days later armed with his new creation: the Pontoon Hopper. Bill Blades and Dave Whitlock would have been green with envy. It looked more like a hopper than the real thing, but Vince found out looks weren't everything when the new creation cast like a bear. Undaunted and even more determined, he set out in quest of the elusive brown. With effort and a little change in casting technique, Vince was able to control the new hopper.

There was no trouble in locating the quarry. Charlie would go upstream, throw a few hoppers on the water from a preselected vantage point, and observe the feeding trout. He would then relay instructions to Vince. This strategy worked well. The first encounter would have been considered a victory for the average angler, but not for Vince. Charlie brought the trout up with hoppers and they could both see it. Charlie's upstream position enabled him to watch the trout as it rose and keep Vince informed. The first test of the new hopper was at hand. Vince cast, placing the imitation perfectly, and Charlie watched it touch the water and start its journey downstream. As it came into the trout's window, the fish inched toward the surface, drifted backward with the fly, followed it for about three feet, nosed down, and swam to its original feeding station. The next half-dozen casts produced the same results: look, follow, and reject. Charlie was ecstatic, but not Vince.

For the next few weeks every encounter was the same.

Finally one morning the climax was at hand, though neither angler knew what was about to happen. As always, Charlie went upstream to his watching station. Vince cast while Charlie relayed instructions. The trout rose to the hopper and began its backward drift and inspection. Vince anticipated the usual reaction, but suddenly the nose broke the water, the hopper was inhaled, and Vince reacted. He realized at once that the weight and strength of the huge brown were far more than he and Charlie had estimated. They had guessed the trout to be twenty-six to twenty-eight inches and seven or eight pounds. Vince now knew they were wrong.

The trout headed for the cover of the deep channel and protection of the weed. For what seemed like an eternity, it couldn't be moved. Vince was certain the leader had become so tangled in the weeds that it was only a matter of time until the shaking and surging of the brown would break it. Suddenly, the pressure lightened and the trout began to move upstream. Vince arched the bamboo rod, turning the fish midstream. The trout was moved to the center of the deep channel. Thoughts of victory, I'm sure, flashed through Vince's mind. The pressure from the rod lifted the trout near the surface, giving Charlie and Vince their first close-up look at the fish. It was much deeper in body than either had realized. Charlie had moved downstream and Vince upstream when suddenly, with strong strokes of the huge tail, the brown began to bore for the bottom. Vince applied all the pressure he could, but the trout continued to dive for cover. It finally made it to the undercut bank, shaking its huge head violently and sending throbbing impulses along the line and into Vince's rod. Vince felt the line go slack, and just as suddenly as the fight had begun, it ended. Though he would have liked to land the trout, measure it, weigh it, and return it to the river, Vince felt satisfied. After two frustrating seasons, he had become the victor. He felt relieved and could look forward to future encounters.

I mentioned earlier that Charlie could bring the trout up with hoppers. As with the beetle feeding, we also had hopper-feeding episodes. The meadows and fields were loaded from July to October. Charlie had a huge boat net on which he replaced the bag with a fine netting. He would walk through the grass, making large sweeping circles. He would collect three- to four-dozen hoppers at one time. They would be picked from the net and placed into a live box or jar. Then, off to the water he would go, pick a spot, and toss a half-dozen or so hoppers, one at a time, about two or three feet from the bank.

Immediately the hoppers began hectic kicking and swimming motions to reach the bank. They wouldn't drift more than a few feet before the gulping trout would start. You could then walk downstream and go to work with your imitation. It was exciting but exasperating. If you were lucky, you might fool one of a half-dozen hopper-eaters. It was amazing how we could feed those trout day after day, week after week, and only fool the few we did.

It was during those early years that Ernie Schweibert became a regular weekend visitor to Charlie's meadow. Ernie, one of the most accomplished fly fishermen I'd ever met, loved the challenge of the Letort's browns. His success ratio of trout hooked and released for numbers fished over was phenomenal. Charlie says Ernie's initial reaction to the beetle and hopper feeding was one of suspicion. He figured that the live insects gave the angler the advantage, but after several excursions he began to agree with Charlie that it was not much of an advantage after all.

I watched one morning as Charlie led Ernie into the upper section of the meadow for a go at the hopper feeders. As usual, Charlie collected the hoppers, positioned Ernie along the bank, and went upstream to start the game. Charlie started a line of hoppers and told Ernie to just watch and locate the trout. As the hoppers floated downstream, five fish were located and their positions memorized. Charlie started a second flotilla. Ernie went to work on the risers and by the time he finished he had hooked and released every trout that had shown. To my knowledge, that was the one and only time a performance like that had taken place. Ernie had tied a hopper imitation that worked well. It was a #14, as I recall, tied on a 1X or 2X Long hook. It had a yellow body, turkey wing tied in a muddler style, a full deer-hair wing over the body, and clipped deer-hair head. After that everyone started tying Ernie's imitation.

Ed Shenk of Carlisle, Pennsylvania, worked the Geological Survey in the mid-1950s. He lived in Washington, D.C., during the week, but his weekends were spent on the Letort, Big Spring, and Falling Spring during terrestrial season. One weekend Ed and I were fishing the Letort on a Saturday morning. We started just above Charlie's, alternating working on the trout we spotted. We were both using hoppers. An hour or more later and halfway through the upper section of the Letort, Ed's count was five or six trout to one of mine. Admittedly, Ed knew these trout and this water better than I, and his casting ability far surpassed mine in those early years, but this was ridiculous.

Catching up with Ed, I asked, "What are you using?"

"Hopper," he calmly answered.

"What size tippet?"

"5X."

He turned and cautiously moved away from the water's

edge. Looking up, he had that cat-that-ate-the-canary grin from ear to ear. "Uh oh," I thought, "I've been had again. He's no more using a hopper than he is a worm." Holding the fly in his clenched hand, he walked over and opened his hand, exposing his hopper. Shocked, I muttered, "That's what I've got on."

"Not quite," came his answer, along with another one of those grins. I'd about had it. The fly looked just like Ernie's hopper.

Holding the hopper close enough for me to see, Ed said, "Look at the turkey wing."

"Well, I'll be," was all I could mumble. The wing was tied flat over the body beneath the deer-hair wing.

"You mean *that's* the difference?" I queried.

"I'm certain. I've been using it since last season and the results have been great," he answered. Reaching into his fly box, he handed me one of his "secret" hoppers. The last half of the morning was the exact opposite of what had happened to me in the previous two hours. Shenk's hopper really worked.

On the way back down to Charlie's meadow at the end of the morning's fishing, Ed related to me the logic behind his hopper pattern. The wing tied flat over the body gave a more definite silhouette when viewed from beneath, more like the broad square-shaped body of the real hopper. The deer-hair tips of the wing above the flat turkey wing produced the semblance of legs as the fly lay in the surface film, and looking at it later from underneath in a glass dish of water was proof enough for me.

Some years later when we were in the shop together, Ed and I had Lefty Kreh take some underwater shots of the imitation and natural. The similarity between the silhouettes was remarkable. Lefty shot all the terrestrials on water for a presentation we made to Orvis, hoping they would carry the flies in their catalog. G. Dick Finlay of Orvis agreed whole-heartedly and the following year, 1960-1961, the Letort Brand terrestrial selection made the catalog.

Another story worth telling comes to mind. It took place a number of years later, in 1967. Upon graduation from Mansfield State College, Tony Skilton accepted a teaching position in Potter County in the north-central part of Pennsylvania. He rented a small cottage between Gaines and Galeton, smack in the middle of what Pennsylvanians call "God's Country." A local lad who was an avid fisherman and hunter wound up as Tony's roommate for three years. He introduced Tony to every piece of water worth knowing about in Potter County, and not only the well-known and famous waters, but every small brook and tributary that held trout. In return, Tony tied flies for him and taught him all he knew about limestone fishing techniques. The match-up produced spectacular results.

During that first winter, through phone calls, letters, and occasional visits back to Boiling Springs, Tony rambled on and on about the fantastic fishing from June through September with terrestrials, not only on the dozens of well-known trout waters, but especially on the small feeder streams. He told of hundreds of trout caught and released, from native brookies to streambred browns to trophy trout taken in water perhaps six feet to twenty feet wide, where these little-known feeders fed the major watersheds. I must have heard "You've got to come up and try this" a thousand or more times that winter.

Understand, as young, eager, and enthusiastic as Tony was, he was not one to stretch or exaggerate his trouting experiences even a little bit, a quality not always found among the fishing fraternity. You may perhaps have known one or two over the years who fall into the "not always" category.

By March I couldn't take it any longer. I'd fished Potter County over the years, but always in the early spring when the water was "right," as the locals put it. I never experienced anything the likes of what Tony described. So, I told him I would come up and camp for a week after the July fourth madness was over. He made arrangements at a local hotel about a mile from his place with four campsites. I couldn't wait for April to turn to July.

When we entered Potter County the anticipation really started to build. The last twenty miles to Tony's reminded me of my anticipation, as a young lad, of opening day. He and his tales of trout really had me wound up.

The following morning Tony joined me for breakfast—a quick breakfast, I must admit—the trout were waiting! We hadn't driven a mile past Tony's house when he said, "Pull in the next dirt road to the right after we cross a little stream." Crossing the water, I looked out of the window on Tony's side to check it out. It couldn't have been fifteen feet wide and looked very, very low. We turned in the dirt road and then Tony instructed me to pull into the little clearing on the right and I did just that. We got out of the station wagon, walked around, and opened the back, all the while looking through the brush to get a glimpse of the water.

"You sure this is it?" I asked hesitantly.

"Yep. It's a little way between the pools the trout move into when the big river warms up, but you're not going to believe what you'll run into," came his reply.

"What should we start with?" Again, I asked hesitantly.

"Try a hopper, size #14 on a 5X tippet. I don't think these trout ever saw a fisherman up here and doubt that they'd ever seen an artificial fly until John brought me here last summer," Tony answered.

We were both using 6-foot rods and Tony recommended a 7 1/2-foot leader. Most casts would be fifteen to twenty feet maximum. Twenty yards or so from the wagon we were on the stream, fast with lots of broken water and the occasional pool. It looked good, but I was still uncertain.

"Let me start and fish for a short distance in the bottom section. I'll point out where to place the fly and the kind of pools in which the trout hold. It gets better the farther up we go," Tony stated confidently.

He took a step or two into the brook (that's what I would have called it), and began to false-cast with about fifteen feet of line and leader. He let the line go and the hopper dropped into a narrow channel of fast water that flowed into a little pool no larger than a sofa cushion. The fly no sooner hit the water than there was a splash and the hopper disappeared. The trout was a five- or six-inch brookie. It acted like it hadn't had a meal in a week. Releasing the trout, Tony took a few more steps, cast again on a little piece of broken water, and an eight-inch brown came to his net. He continued his routine, and in less than twenty yards had released seven beautiful streambred trout. I watched in amazement as Tony calmly talked his way through the entire happening.

"Okay, you try it," Tony said, stepping onto the bank. "I'll talk you through the first go-round." Following Tony's example, I stepped into the water and began to work out line. As though I'd turned on a recording, Tony's instructions came from the bank. "See that rock, drop the fly in the little chute going to that pool to your right in that pocket on the bank," as though he were teaching a class for the hundredth time. I hadn't covered as much water as he had, and released four trout and cleanly missed two others. This was hard to believe.

"Let's head upstream to the first good pool," Tony's voice interrupted my relaxed, contented, and satisfied state of mind. "There's a sixteen-inch brown that feeds near the tail-end of the pool. He's been there every trip I've made here. He spooks easily, but can be fooled." Tony led the way as we headed upstream. Stopping suddenly, he pointed to the tail of a pool perhaps twenty feet wide and thirty feet long. The water looked quite shallow in the tail. Hunching over, we worked closer, covering the last ten feet on our knees. Tony scanned the water until he located the trout. Showing me the brown, he again began instructing. "False-cast and get the distance, then drop the fly two feet in front and a foot to the left of the brown." The first cast was almost perfect. The trout turned to his left, came up under the hopper, and drifted along for a foot or so. Casually, he turned and swam to his original feeding position. The second cast didn't even get a look, and the third cast sent him scurrying for cover.

The next hour or more was unbelievable. Between us we released twenty-three trout from five to fourteen inches. "What do you think?" Tony asked, as we headed down the road to the station wagon.

"This is unbelievable," was the only reply I could muster.

"Wait," he said, "The next one is even better."

We drove another two miles, turned again to the right, and parked the wagon. This time we took turns. Tony went first, so I could observe his tactics. We hopscotched the stream for perhaps a little more than a mile before it narrowed to a trickle. The result was twenty-seven trout between us, a few in the twelve- to fourteen-inch class, but most between six and eight inches. It was well past lunch so we headed back to camp. We hadn't been four miles up the road.

After dinner that evening I visited with Tony. As much as I didn't want it to be, the better part of the evening's conversation was on what lay ahead for the rest of the week. Tony assured me the fishing would be even better. How? He said that perhaps two dozen or more streams just like the two on which we spent that day were within a forty-minute drive of his place. He was right. That week was one of the most memorable I'd ever experienced.

In the early 1980s I spent a week in Manchester, Vermont. I visited with Tony frequently. Tony was then director of the Orvis Fishing Schools and because he worked the schools Friday, Saturday, and Sunday during the summer, he had Mondays and Tuesdays off.

On Monday and Tuesday of that week Tony took me on a tour of several mountain streams he had been fishing for several years, small streams that were loaded with brook or brown trout. We didn't spend a lot of time fishing because Tony's intent was to show me the waters and be sure I could find my way back to them during the course of the week. I was able to find them on my own, and in four days of fishing caught and released more trout in those mountain brooks on terrestrials than even Tony could believe. I used crickets, hoppers, ants, and beetles, and the Letort Hopper in size #14 out-produced all the other patterns.

One small brook intrigued me more than any of the others. About a third of the way up the mountain the brook ran through a farm for half a mile. It looked more like a meandering meadow limestone stream in Pennsylvania than a Vermont mountain brook. It was no more than twenty feet across at its widest point and was supposed to be full of brown trout. I fished it the second day I was on my own and hooked and released fifteen trout in about two hours, all on a Letort Hopper.

The following day I fished a stream that Tony claimed was full of streambred rainbows. I fished the lower section, a little more than a mile of it, as it meandered its way through the prettiest meadows I'd seen in Vermont. Every pool, pocket, and riffle held one, two, and often a half-dozen trout. By the time I'd fished my way back to the car I'd released just short of two-dozen rainbows. Nothing big, but all scrappy and very healthy. They were taken on Letort Hoppers, size #14.

After lunch I decided to fish upstream through a heavily wooded section that Tony told me had some deep pools and excellent pocket water. He said it was about half a mile to the next bridge upstream and it would be easy to walk the road back to the car. By the time I reached the first deep pool, I had hooked and released four trout on the hopper. The pool yielded only one fish, but it was a good one for the size of the stream. A heavy fourteen-inch rainbow was on my line, again on a Letort Hopper. By the time I reached the bridge, I'd returned seven more rainbows to the water. I fished a quarter mile or so above the bridge and the stream took on the characteristics of a typical mountain brook: faster water, riffles, a few pockets, and no pools. Three more rainbows succumbed to the #14 hopper.

It was a fantastic week. As I drove home, I reflected on the week's happenings. It finally began to sink in that the terrestrials were every bit as effective on freestone water as they were on limestoners. What was born of necessity on the banks of the Letort during the 1950s was destined to become a boon to fly fishermen from Maine to California. Fate works in mysterious ways.

Charlie Fox, the "Gentleman Host of the Letort," on his meadow in 1962.

Joe Brooks and Ed Koch on Falling Spring, 1960.

A — Gallery of Letort Regulars

Ed Shenk and Lefty Kreh in Charlie Fox's meadow in 1962.

Lee Wulff and Ed Koch at a meeting of the Harrisburg Fly Fishers in 1962.

The great Joe Brooks at a meeting of the Brotherhood of the Junglecock, 1964.

A master of the Letort: Ed Shenk with an 8 1/2-pound brown taken from the Letort in 1964.

Norm Shires and Charlie Fox on a Letort meadow in 1980.

Joe Brooks and Tony Skilton in 1964.

A Gallery of Letort Regulars

Ed Shenk on the Yellow Breeches in 1981.

Ed Koch on the Yellow
Breeches, 1988.

(Inset) Don Dubois,
Ross Trimmer, and
Charlie Fox on the
Letort, 1986.

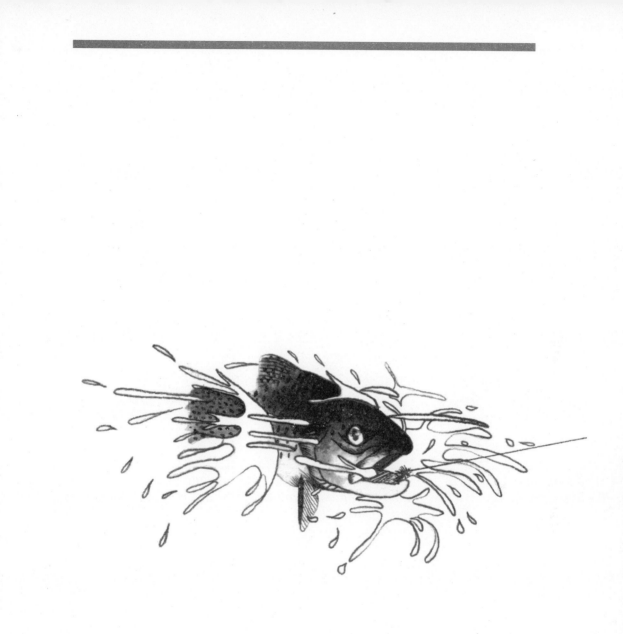

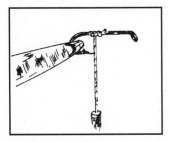

1. Insert hook in vise and attach thread directly above hook point.

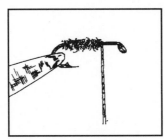

2. Dub fur body from bend of hook two-thirds the length of the shank toward the hook eye.

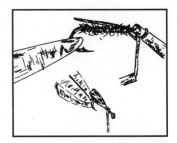

3. Tie wing on flat along the top of hook shank. Half-hitch thread. The wing should end just above hook bend.

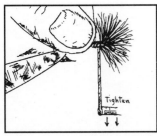

7. Pull thread tight. The hair will begin to flare.

8. Wind thread forward through the hair, flaring it as you wind. Tie off at hook eye.

9. Whip-finish.

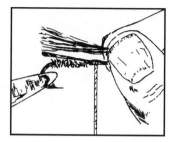

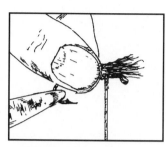

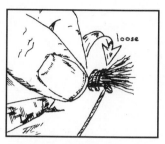

4. Clip a bunch of deer hair. Measure hair along hook shank for proper length, which should be the length of the flat wing.

5. Hold hair on top of hook shank with thumb and forefinger.

6. Wrap two loose turns of thread at the front of the hook and around the hair bunch.

10. Clip fly head to desired shape. Clip closely; most beginners leave the head too large. Clip the top, sides, and bottom of the hair that extends over the wing.

11. Apply head cement, and the fly is complete.

The Letort Hopper

Hook: #14, #16, or #18 (Mustad 9671, Tiemco 2312)

Thread: Brown

Body: Dubbed fur—yellow, cream, or tan

Wing: Mottled turkey or hen pheasant

Head and Overwing: Deer or elk hair

The Cricket

5

With the development of the hopper, fishing activity along the Letort returned to some semblance of order. The newly developed Jassids, beetles, ants, and hoppers filled a void that had plagued Letort anglers for almost twenty years. No longer were endless hours spent at the tying bench in search of successful patterns. No longer were there frustrating, fishless days astream.

Instead, from June to September an angler knew he could spend several hours, or the entire day, in pursuit of surface-feeding Letort brooks and browns armed with the new terrestrial patterns. Depending on the angler's skill, he could be certain of at least several, and oftentimes numerous, successful encounters with the previously "untouchable" free-risers. I don't think any of the Letort regulars in those days were really aware of how true Joe Brooks's statement in *Outdoor Life* was when he wrote: "Terrestrial fishing has opened up a whole new area for the fly fisherman."

For several years the success of the new terrestrial patterns spread rapidly among eastern anglers. Every weekend saw an ever-increasing number of fly fishers seeking out Carlisle, Pennsylvania, and the famous Letort limestoner. Many of these early visitors were content to observe the regulars or spend hours on the benches in Charlie Fox's meadow listening to fishing tales from Charlie, Vince Marinaro, Don Dubois, Ernie Schweibert, Norm Lightner, Ed Shenk, Tommy Thomas, Ross Trimmer, Frank Honisch, Gene Utech, Lefty Kreh, Gene Shetter, Jim Chesney, Chuck Kissinger, and others. Not one of those early participants had the vaguest idea what lay ahead for Carlisle's Cumberland Valley—its waters, its fly fishermen, and the impact they would make on American fly fishing.

I opened a small fly shop and mail-order business in 1959, and catered to local fly fishermen and the few visitors who fished the area. At that time there were few shops strictly for fly fishermen and still fewer to carry fly-tying supplies. Ernie Hille in Williamsport, Pennsylvania, and Herters were our major sources of supply. Within one short season I became deluged with orders, letters, and phone calls for the new terrestrial flies and the materials to tie them. At the end of two years I was selling flies and materials to Orvis, Abercrombie and Fitch, William Mills, Flatbrook Ernie (New Jersey), Bud Lilly, Buz Buzsek in California, and a dozen or so fly shops scattered across the county. By the end of the third season, Cumberland County was selling more new resident fishing licenses than any other county in the state. Hard as it is to believe, we still were not aware of what was taking place and the part it would play in fly-fishing history.

I can't be certain when or where the following incident took place, but would be inclined to say it happened while Ed Shenk and I were working in my shop in the early

1960s. Ed had been having a better than average run of luck, or rather, success, on his early morning outings on the Letort. He would go out about 6 or 6:30 a.m. and fish until 8:30 or so and be back at the shop by 9:00 a.m. I was certain this success was not happenstance. Ed knew the Letort and every trout in it better than anyone in those days. He should have; he spent more hours on it than any other regular. One morning we talked about fishing for a while, but Ed did not give an indication that anything new or unusual was taking place. Suddenly, without a word, Ed walked out to his car and came back with one of his many fly boxes in hand. There it was, that half smile-half smirk as he walked toward the counter. I should have known that he had come up with something; something he had not shared with any of the fly fishermen he knew. Opening the box, he picked out a fly and laid it on the counter.

"What's that?", was all I could muster, not wanting to appear uninformed (that sounds better than dumb, which is what I was) while looking at what appeared to be a black deer-hair hopper on the counter. I couldn't for the life of me figure out why anyone would want to tie a black hopper.

"It's a cricket," came his reply. Nothing more—no explanation, no reason. He was waiting for me to ask.

"Does it work? Why, how did you come up with it?" I asked, praying he would fill me in on the details.

His reply was lengthy, detailed, and explicit. One has to know Ed Shenk to understand what makes him tick. Whether it's trout fishing, grouse or deer hunting, or trapping, Ed teeters on the verge of fanaticism. This trait, however, is his secret of success. He doesn't miss a trick, astream or afield. He can think like a trout, grouse, deer, fox, or muskrat, and as a result comes out the winner. Out of this intensity came the now-famous Letort Cricket.

Others had figured out the secrets of the Jassid, floating ant, beetles, and hoppers, and the results seemed obvious. Terrestrials abounded in unbelievable numbers in the meadows along the Letort; they got into the water and the trout loved them—logical cause-and-effect. The only problem was that when Charlie, Vince, and others got to number four, the hopper, they quit. For them, the battle was won. They had emerged victorious, and rightfully so. But this was not enough for Ed Shenk. From the day he cast his first fly (about forty five years ago or more), Ed has never stopped searching, innovating, and developing new patterns. The cricket is just one of many. When he fishes, he fishes hard, harder than most fly fishermen I know. To follow him for six or eight hours on the stream is an experience one cannot easily forget. In spite of his intensity while fishing he still has the ability to observe everything going on about him, whether in or on the water. So, his discovery of the cricket really came as no surprise. In fact, he had tied and fished the cricket with phenomenal success the previous season. Not only had he proven its worth on the Letort, but on Big Spring, Falling Spring, Green Spring, Yellow Breeches, Spring Creek (then known as Fisherman's Paradise), and more than a dozen other favorites he regularly fished but never talked about. The cricket was the final pattern of the soon-to-be-famous Letort terrestrials.

I had the opportunity to fish the new fly perhaps a dozen times or so in the months following Ed's showing it to me. It was unreal. If a difficult hopper-eater was encountered and couldn't be touched no matter how cautious the approach, how perfect the presentation, without fail he could be taken with the new cricket imitation. It was only about six weeks after Ed had given me the pattern that I made arrangements to fish one Sunday morning with a group of fly fishermen from Ohio who had been spending every weekend during July and August for several seasons camping in Charlie's meadow and partaking of the trout and the camaraderie of the regulars.

As usual, I was up before daylight, had eggs, toast, and coffee, checked my fly boxes, and drove across town to Charlie's meadow. I pulled on my waders, slipped into my vest, grabbed my 6-foot 1-piece Orvis, and headed for the tent that was less than fifty yards from the car. The Ohio boys hadn't begun to stir, so I woke them, and told them to have some breakfast and that I would meet them upstream later on. Fate had to be smiling on me that day, for less than an hour later I was back at the tent with a twenty-seven and one-half-inch nine-pound brown trout taken on a #12 Letort Cricket. (More later in Chapter 7.)

During those early years, Joe Brooks became a frequent visitor and guest of Charlie Fox. As a result, Ed and I began to tie dozens of the new terrestrial patterns for him. He fished them all over the world and kept Charlie, Ed, and me informed of the success he had with them. The hopper and the cricket became two of his favorites. On a salmon-fishing trip he proudly reported taking a salmon on a cricket. On his early trips to Argentina the crickets and hoppers were equally successful.

During 1970, 1971, and 1972, Dick Wood from New Jersey visited my Yellow Breeches Angler fly shop regularly. Dick was in the advertising business and one of his major accounts was the Fenwick company. I had met Dick in the late 1950s when he was a manufacturer's representative for Gudebrod and Penn reels. We bought a lot of Gudebrod thread from him in those days. He loved to fish the Falling Spring near Chambersburg, Pennsylvania, during July and August. He would spend many mornings fishing the then-famous Trico hatch. By late morning he would head to the dairy story near the headwaters to have a huge plate of ice cream topped off with an extra large milk shake, the combination readying him for an afternoon of tempting the streambred rainbows of Falling Spring with crickets. It was not unusual for Dick to catch and release upwards of a dozen trout during an afternoon working crickets. A feat, I might add, not often accomplished by most of the locals, myself included.

Watching Dick work those oftentimes unyielding, demanding, challenging streambred rainbows, I wondered for years how he ever managed to catch the first one. His casting technique looked awful—sloppy, careless, and a dozen other adjectives I can't even think of. No matter, he continued to catch trout. I would become so frustrated watching such a flagrant display of how *not* to cast, that I would head off upstream not wanting other anglers to even think I knew such a klutz. In spite of all these feelings, I was intrigued with Dick's trout-catching abilities. By all the rules of the game he should have been skunked each and every day he set foot astream, but he wasn't.

There was one section of Falling Spring that held a good number of better-than-average-size trout. The stream passed under a bridge and ran rapidly for sixty yards or so in a typical deep channel before it opened into a placid pool about thirty feet wide and eighty to ninety feet long. A third of the way below the head of the pool willow trees on both banks covered the entire width and branches hung to within two feet of the water's surface. It was in this protected haven that the trout took refuge and fed, undisturbed by any angler, all day long. Out of frustration, perhaps even desperation, wanting to see Dick skunked just *one* time, I led him upstream to the Willow Hole.

Terrestrial Fishing

As we approached the tail of the pool I stopped Dick and told him to watch under the branches that covered the stream about two-thirds of the way up the pool. Sure enough, there they were, four trout cruising and rising regularly, each of them in a feeding circle no more than three feet in diameter. They were respectable trout, from twelve to sixteen inches. Dick watched for a few minutes as the fish continued their metronomic feeding. "You can get in the water here, wade very carefully, and maneuver yourself into a good casting position," I calmly told him. As he slowly moved into the tail of the pool, I began to gloat. I didn't know anyone, visitor or regular, myself included, who had mastered this situation and was able with any consistency to get a cast to, much less fool, these particular trout. I ignored twinges of guilt as I watched my friend prepare for what I was certain would be inevitable defeat. A solid trouncing of an angler by four untouchable trout! Had anyone else been with me that day I would have briskly advised him of the correct state of affairs. But I settled down contentedly on the bank to watch.

As I had expected, Dick began to false-cast, working out line, measuring the distance needed to reach the still-feeding trout. Several times he dropped his fly on the placid surface well behind the trout and the overhanging willow branches. Each time the line drifted on the water Dick stripped a few feet from the reel and shook it through the guides. Really confused by his antics, I watched as Dick picked the line from the water, made a beautiful backcast, and came forward ready to place his fly under the willow branches, or so I thought. The loop turned over beautifully, pulling the slack fly line through the guides. Suddenly, Dick stopped the line with his left hand, his fly landing some three feet behind the nearest trout. "Aha," I thought, watching his fly begin to drift downstream, "He has finally realized the predicament he's in. This is going to be tough." Dick raised his rod, following the drifting line and stopping it at the one o'clock position as if preparing for another cast. Suddenly he drove the rod tip forward hard and made the most beautiful roll cast I'd ever seen. His line rolled over perfectly, the leader turned in a tight loop, and the size #14 cricket attached to the twenty-four-inch 5X tippet sailed under the willow limbs and landed just six inches from the trout farthest back. The instant the fly touched the water the trout turned and without any hesitation whatever took Dick's cricket as though it had been waiting all day for that particular fly to drift by. Dick struck and with one motion set the hook and turned the trout's head downstream. The trout never had the chance to move even an inch upstream from the spot where he inhaled the black imitation. The upper three trout were never disturbed.

"Nice job," I mumbled, as Dick's hand slid down the tippet, grasped the fly, and released a fourteen-inch brown without ever lifting its head from the water. I was stunned, flabbergasted, angry, and impressed all at the same time. I couldn't believe what I had just witnessed. To make matters worse, Dick proceeded to take the remaining three trout identically as he had taken the first, with roll casts! Wading toward the bank where I sat, he commented, "That was neat. Are there any more spots like that up here?" I cringed and he knew it as he continued to comment on how easy these Falling Spring trout were. "Was it okay that I used a roll cast on them?" he asked, sitting down beside me in the grass. "I know it wasn't the proper way to cast to them, but I know I could never have gotten my fly under those willows with an overhand cast like I was supposed to." He was referring to our (the limestone regulars') "proper" approach toward these redoubtable trout.

Now, as sarcastic as I may sound, I learned a hard lesson that day, as I have on many occasions from the anglers I've been fortunate enough to spend time with. Every lesson I learned from those dozens of angling companions over the last thirty years has contributed more to the success I enjoy as a fly fisherman than I can ever convey.

I don't know why or whatever possessed me to think of it or to try to do it, but one season I made up my mind to attempt to take a trout with a floating cricket on opening day on the Yellow Breeches. The first season I tried was 1972. I found that by midmorning, or noon at the latest, the sun, if there was any, warmed up the west bank of the river enough that several trout could be found feeding close to the bank along the overhanging brush. Some would be surface feeding, others subsurface, but all were close enough to the top that any insect drifting by could be seen and taken with ease. Using a size #16 Letort Cricket, which was small enough to fool a trout into thinking it was one of the small black caddis that come off all year, I had no trouble in duping three trout that first season into taking the tiny black terrestrial. For eight years I was able to catch and release a trout on a floating cricket on that day.

Another cricket incident happened late in August of 1972, again on the Yellow Breeches. It involved Norm Shires, my photographer friend and angling companion. We had decided to meet one Sunday afternoon and fish the upper half-mile of the fly area. I had located a number of good trout over twenty inches during the course of the season and felt sure that we might have a chance of locating one or more of them if there hadn't been too many anglers wading up and down that section. Starting at the deep water just above Allenberry and fishing the right-hand bank covered with huge overhanging buttonwood trees for a quarter-mile or more, we each caught and released a half-dozen or so trout, Norm on his usual ants, and I on a #14 cricket.

I had just maneuvered my way around twenty yards of huge boulders at the head of the deep water and stopped in the beginning of a fast stretch to watch for feeding activity. It was a beautiful, brilliant afternoon. The river was low and gin-clear. Every trout in a feeding position or lie could be seen with Polaroid glasses as far as ten feet from the far bank. It was a day worth being on the river, trout or not. Two small fish were feeding regularly just at the edge of a wild rose bush that grew out over the water. Edging my way slowly to midstream, I dropped the size #16 cricket just a few inches to the left of the closest trout. The cricket no sooner touched the water than the trout turned midstream and drew in the imitation so subtly that the ring was almost imperceptible. I raised the rod tip abruptly and the brownie turned, dove, and headed for the cover of the rose bush. In a matter of minutes a plump ten-inch brown came to net. The capture of trout number two was almost identical.

I looked downstream to see how Norm was doing. He was working on a consistent riser with his ant, and three casts later he fooled him. Turning back upstream, I worked my way closer to the right-hand bank and headed upstream around the rose bush. About three feet beyond the bush I stopped to search the water upstream. About fifteen feet in front of my position and not a foot from the bank a small brown was cruising the shallow water, sipping intently. A few feet in front of him another brown lay in his feeding station in front of a basketball-size rock. Ten feet in front of the second trout I spotted three more trout just on the edge of the fast water, feeding on nymphs. This had become standard procedure for me over the years: get into position and search the water for trout as far upstream as can be seen. Then, start to work the closest trout and slowly continue upstream through the others. Five feet in front of the nymphing trout the remains of an old tree trunk lay submerged about four feet from the bank in the calm water. It was always a dependable spot to find a feeding trout.

Eyes straining to see into the water, not just at it, I must have stood for a full five minutes looking for any movement, any shape that might be a trout, anything that would confirm the feeling that this was a logical spot for a good fish. My eyes moved toward the edge of the fast water about three feet to the left of the tree trunk. There in the deeper water I could barely make out the silhouette of a fish. It was just far enough into the deep water that the broken surface made it difficult to see. It was well in front of the nearest trout, perhaps thirty feet or more, so I decided to work on the closer fish. I dressed my #16 cricket and dropped it into the calm water between the sipping trout and the bank. The cricket gently touched the water, the brown turned and swam under the fly, inspecting it for a matter of seconds. Seeing its mouth open and the water dimple, I raised the rod. The trout headed for the fast water with the tiny cricket showing from the roof of its snout. A few minutes later a plump brown was in my net.

Drying the fly, I instinctively looked to the submerged log. There it lay between the log and the fast water, a magnificent brown in the eighteen- to twenty-inch class. In minutes it rose once, then a second and third time. This was a common occurrence from August through October on the Yellow Breeches. The water was low and clear. The temperature along the right bank remained ten degrees colder than in midstream and the left bank, as a result of the influx of the fifty-two-degree water from Little Run and the lake just a half-mile upstream, was very cold—a unique combination of circumstances providing a unique fishing environment. Another plus those fifteen years ago was the absence of anglers. The solitude of several hours on the river, the companionship of a friend, the existence of an abundant trout population, all feed the spirit. A hectic work week can soon be forgotten.

Turning downstream, I called softly to Norm, motioning him to join me. As he started upstream, I turned again to watch the big brown. It was feeding on nymphs just under the surface. Occasionally it moved toward the log and sipped something from the top. I eased over to the bank and sat down as Norm reached my earlier position.

"What's up?" he asked quietly.

"Look upstream about thirty to forty feet to that old tree trunk, and about a foot to the left of it," I answered.

Norm scanned the water for a few seconds. Then I heard, "Oh brother, that's a good one."

"He's feeding just under the surface, occasionally sipping something on top. What do you have on?" I asked.

"A size eighteen ant."

"Give him a try and see what happens."

Norm began to work out line carefully, measuring the distance to the brown. His first cast was a perfect landing, a foot in front of the feeding trout. The tiny ant drifted delicately on the surface. The trout's nose tipped up just an inch from the imitation and began drifting back under the fly. Calmly it went down, swimming slowly upstream to its original position. On the next dozen or more casts the trout rose under and followed the fly four more times before refusing.

Reeling in, Norm questioned, "What do you think I should try?"

"Got any crickets?" I asked. He nodded in the affirmative. "Try a size fourteen."

Cutting the ant from the tippet, he tied on a #14 Letort Cricket. Another cast placed the black imitation perfectly in front of and slightly to the left of the brown. As the fly approached, the fish came up under it again, drifted back, and went down.

"Rest him a minute and then try to put the fly on his right side close to the log," I encouraged. "He may be fooled if he thinks the real thing dropped from those overhanging bushes."

Norm calmly watched the fish for a few minutes as it rose twice, sipping something from the surface. He worked out line, measuring the distance, then let the line go, turning over a beautiful tight loop. The leader straightened three feet above the water and the cricket drifted gently down. The instant the fly touched the surface, almost two feet to the right of its head, the monster turned, swam to the fly, rose, and inhaled it without hesitation. The rod rose sharply, sinking the tiny barb into the roof of the brown's upper jaw. Instantly the trout turned, surged for the fast water midstream, and shook its huge head violently, sending throbbing vibrations from the tip to the butt of the delicate 6 1/2-foot Orvis bamboo. Reeling in the slack line, Norm held the trout momentarily in the fast water. "Boy, he feels good," was all Norm could utter. The brown had enough. With a violent shake of its head it turned in the current and headed downstream. Line screamed from Norm's reel. The rod held high and arched and strained against the weight of the fish and the pressure of the fast water. "Better get to the other side if you can. You'll have a better chance to follow him from that side," I suggested.

Slowly, carefully, Norm maneuvered his way to the left

bank and into water that would afford him the advantage should the brown make another run for the refuge of the deep water, some sixty yards below. The trout was holding, at least for a time, about thirty yards below where Norm had hooked it. It appeared the angler had gained the upper hand. I left the bank cautiously, so as not to spook the fish, and worked my way to the far bank. Norm hadn't used a net six times in the past ten years. He felt less damage was done if trout were released without being grabbed or lifted from the water into a net bag. This was one afternoon he regretted that decision. Releasing the clip on my net, I attached it to Norm's vest. "Thanks," he said, not taking his eyes from the spot in the river where his line entered the water. Some twenty minutes had passed.

Norm was able to gain line slowly and move the trout out of the deep channel in the fast water. This was his first opportunity to get a good look at the monster brownie. "My God, he's bigger than twenty inches," he excitedly called as the trout came into the shallow water twenty feet below him. The encounter was coming to an end. The trout continued to surge, trying desperately to regain the safety of the deep water, but with little avail. The delicate 2 1/2-ounce rod had performed admirably. Finally, the valiant brown succumbed to the net. Norm carefully removed the cricket as he held the trout, resting it in the quiet water. I quickly measured and weighed it—22 1/2 inches, 6 1/2 pounds. A few quick pictures and it was returned safely to the edge of the deep water.

The Letort Cricket

Hook: #12 to #16 (Mustad 9671, Tiemco 101)

Thread: Black

Body: Black dubbed fur

Wing: Goose or duck quill, dyed black

Head and Overwing: Black deer hair

Follow the tying instructions for the Letort Hopper. The only differences between these two flies are in hook size and color.

Other Terrestrials

6

Ed Shenk's development and introduction of the Letort Cricket brought to an end a decade of searching, observation, tying, trying, and finalizing five fly patterns that changed fly tying and fly fishing for the generation of anglers that followed. The Jassid, ants, beetles, hopper, and cricket have been acclaimed some of America's greatest contributions to fly fishing. Over the years I have been asked to try various patterns developed by fly tiers and fly fishermen from all parts of the country. The patterns that follow are only a few, mainly terrestrials that have proven to be exceptional trout-takers. To the best of my knowledge, none was originated in the Cumberland Valley. I mention the names of the fly fishermen who gave them to me, although I cannot state with certainty they were the originators of the patterns. These flies have worked well for me over the years, and each deserves a compartment in every fly box.

The deer-hair and fluorescent yarn inchworm patterns were given to me by Jim Gilson of Angling Fantasies, in Mifflintown, Pennsylvania. The two Live Body Inchworms were first shown to me by Jack Mickievicz of Jack's Tackle, then in Phoenixville, Pennsylvania. The Live Body Beetle imitation is by Jack Mickievicz also. The Para-ant was given to me by Frank Angelo, of Lititz, Pennsylvania.

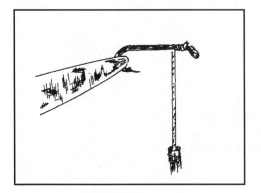

1. *Insert hook in vise and attach thread at front of hook shank, just behind the hook eye.*

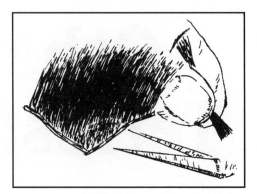

2. *Clip a small bunch of hair, about 1/6- to 1/8-inch thick.*

The Deer-Hair Inchworm

Hook: #12 to #16 (Mustad 9672, Tiemco 2312)

Thread: Green

Body: Dyed green deer or elk hair

5. *Continuing to hold hair between thumb and forefinger, wrap thread toward the rear of the hook as if you were ribbing with tinsel.*

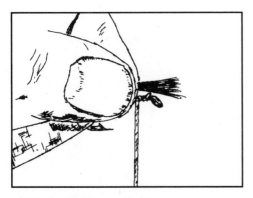

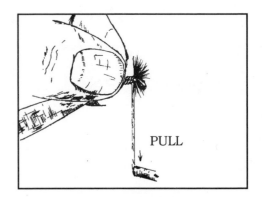

3. Hold hair bunch between thumb and forefinger. Trim hair ends that will face the front of the hook. Place hair on top of hook shank.

4. Wrap two loose turns of thread over hair. Pull thread tight. The hair ends will flare; this is all right.

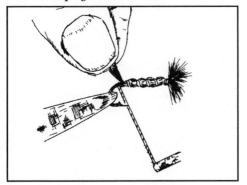

6. When you reach the end of the straight portion of shank, make several wraps of thread under the "tail" of hair and around the hook shank. Half-hitch to secure thread.

7. Wind thread to hook eye, again as if you were ribbing. Tie off. Whip-finish.

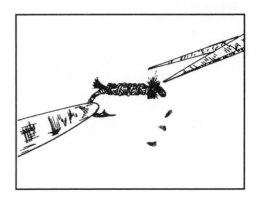

8. Trim the small tuft of flared hair at the head. Apply head cement and the fly is complete.

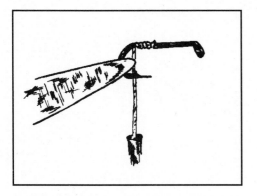

1. Insert hook in vise and attach thread at rear of hook shank where hook begins to bend.

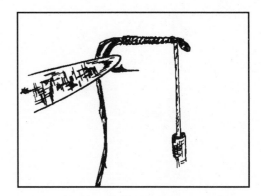

2. Cut a piece of yarn about 4 inches long. Tie in yarn at hook bend. Wrap thread forward to hook eye. Half-hitch.

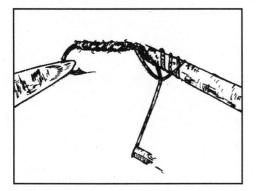

3. Wrap yarn forward from bend of hook to the eye, forming a smooth body. Tie off and clip excess yarn. Whip-finish.

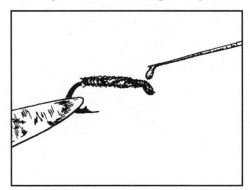

4. Apply head cement, and the fly is complete.

Yarn Inchworm

Hook: #12 to #16

Thread: Green

Body: Green poly yarn or fluorescent yarn

Live Body Inchworm

Hook: Mustad 94831 L/S Dry

Thread: Light green 6/0

Body: Live Body green foam, 1/16-inch

Live Body Hump Inchworm

Hook: Mustad 94831 L/S Dry

Thread: Light green 6/0

Body: Live Body green foam, 1/16-inch

1. Insert hook in vise.
2. Start thread at hook eye and wrap thread backwards the entire length of the shank, to the beginning of the bend.
3. Tie in the foam at the rear of the hook. Leave a small extension of the body beyond the hook bend.
4. Tie the body down, ribbing thread to hook eye. Let the foam body extend beyond the hook eye.
5. Whip-finish the head under the foam body.
6. Clip the foam body 1/4-inch beyond the hook eye. The fly is complete.

1. Insert hook in vise.
2. Start thread at the rear of the hook shank.
3. Tie in foam body at the hook rear. Let 1/4-inch of the body hang over the hook bend.
4. Wind thread to the front of the hook. Cover entire shank with thread.
5. Push the foam body up, gently, to form a hump on top of the hook shank.
6. Tie off the foam body. Leave a small head.
7. Whip-finish, and the fly is complete.

Live Body Beetle

Hook: #12 to #14
(Mustad 94840)

Thread: Black 6/0 or 8/0

Body: Live Body black
(1/8-inch)

Body Center: Live Body
white (1/16-inch)

1. Insert hook in vise. Tie thread in at rear of hook shank.
2. Cut one end of black Live Body on a 45-degree angle.
3. Tie in at rear of hook on one side of shank.
4. Form a loop with black Live Body that extends the length of the hook shank.
5. Tie in white Live Body on top of hook just in front of black Live Body loop.
6. Wrap thread two thirds of the way up hook shank.
7. Fold black Live Body loop forward on top of shank into an oval shape and tie off.
8. Pull white Live Body over the top of the black Live Body loop. The white should fill the gap in the loop of black. Tie off with a half-hitch.
9. Cut black and white Live Body material even with hook eye.
10. Whip-finish, and the fly is complete.

The Para-ant

Hook: #14 to #16
(Mustad 94833, Tiemco
101)

Thread: Black 6/0

Body: Black fur

Hackle: Blue dun

Para-wing: White poly

1. *Insert hook in vise.*
2. *Attach thread above point of barb.*
3. *Dub fur body down over the bend a short distance. Half-hitch. Wrap thread two-thirds of the way up hook shank. Half-hitch.*
4. *Tie in poly wing. Clip off excess. Half-hitch.*
5. *Tie half of front hump, making one wrap of fur in front of poly wing.*
6. *Tie in hackle at front of poly wing.*
7. *Wind hackle four turns around the base of the poly wing. Tie off.*
8. *Clip excess hackle tip.*
9. *Finish off front hump.*
10. *Whip-finish, and the fly is complete.*

A Nine-Pounder

During the trout seasons of 1958, 1959, and 1960 I spent every available hour along the banks of the Letort in pursuit of the wary browns and challenging brookies. When possible, I would meet with Ed Shenk, Charlie Fox, Norm Lightner, Vince Marinaro, and other Letort regulars because their knowledge and expertise taught me more in three short seasons than I could have mastered on my own in a decade. They knew, literally, every trout in the Letort, where it lived, when and where it fed, and the emergences of the mayfly hatches and when terrestrial patterns would be most effective. Most important, they were masters of the techniques necessary for success.

What most amazed me about this group was its willingness to share and teach. I grew up thinking most anglers were obsessively secretive about their knowledge of trout. It took several years for me to fully appreciate the unique fraternity of anglers into which I had been accepted. Each shared his knowledge not only with me, but with any angler who journeyed to the Cumberland Valley. To me they were a rare and happy breed of fly fisherman. For some thirty years now I have been privileged to give back to hundreds of young and not-so-young anglers some of what those early Letort regulars did for me.

During the 1960 and 1961 seasons I located three large trout, six or seven pounds each, I thought. I never found them surface feeding, but always out in feeding pockets in the cress and weed, working cress bugs, shrimp, and sculpins. I was certain that with perseverance I would have one of them.

My encounters with one trout in 1960 numbered well over two dozen, perhaps even closer to three dozen. Because I knew where to find it, it was relatively easy to sneak up and observe as it fed nonchalantly, sometimes for an hour or more. Its lie was all but impenetrable and with every advantage of safety. The pool was on the left bank working upstream. It was about eight to ten feet long, perhaps a yard wide, and made a deep depression in the cress. At the tail end of it a huge hole (to this day I have no idea of its actual size) cut back under the bank, and was the brown's real home. At the slightest indication of danger the trout would drop down and drift casually back to the end of the hole and disappear under the bank. I doubt that two or three out of the hundreds of anglers who trod the banks of the Letort that season were aware of that trout.

Thanks to Ed Shenk's instruction during two previous seasons, particularly his techniques for finding trout and "sneaking" the banks of the Letort, I was able to observe this fish often. One morning during late June in the meadow below the Bonny Brook quarry I found the trophy brown at the head of the hole nosing the cress, drifting back and then side to side, feeding on the cress bugs it dislodged by poking its nose into the weed and shaking its head vigorously. Then it drifted back a few feet and waited for the current to carry the dislodged cress bugs to it. It could feed undisturbed for hours.

My approach on finding the huge brown feeding was always the same. I would drop to my knees in the weeds along the bank and creep and crawl as close as possible. Often I could come within five or ten yards of the feeding monster. It was like watching a child in a play pen. I would kneel and watch for five, ten, even fifteen minutes as the trout enjoyed its leisurely breakfast, trying to determine the line of drift and discover what insects it took most often. I must have made thousands of casts that season and spent hundreds of hours observing. For all that time and effort, I managed to hook him a grand total of three times. No need to tell you who emerged victorious — that trophy brown!

During the 1961 season I worked on two additional trophies, both upstream from my 1960 brown. One lived under the old railroad trestle in the upper section of the Letort; the second made its home in a stretch near the quarry almost at the head of the stream. The second trout's hole offered little protection, making it difficult to get in a good position to work on it and almost impossible to cast without spooking it. I never did manage to hook that one, though I'd find it out feeding regularly.

The fellow under the trestle was another story, however. It fed in a channel in the weed about five feet beyond the concrete abutment, so it was easy to find and rather easy to work on. It lived under the trestle in a hole perhaps ten to fifteen feet wide and twenty to thirty feet long. I never did find out just where it would disappear to when it drifted back into the hole. Not enough sunlight got between the railroad ties to permit my seeing into the depths of the hole.

I hooked the trestle trout and the 1960 brown about seven times each from May to mid-July in 1961. I never came close to getting either to net, no matter how perfect my plan of attack seemed. By the first week of August I began to feel fate did not intend a trophy to hang on the wall of my newly opened fly shop.

During the second week in August I received a phone call from three fishing buddies from Ohio. They were planning a fishing trip for that weekend and wanted to let me know. I arranged to meet them on Sunday morning in the meadow near Charlie Fox's house on the Letort.

Bright and early Sunday I arrived at my friends' tent with my 6 1/2-foot Orvis Flea rigged with a 6X tippet and size #16 cress bug. But my friends were not ready, so while they ate breakfast I wandered downstream to a spot on the stream directly behind Charlie's house. I was surprised not to run into any other fishermen. It took me only a minute or two, standing well back from the bank, to spot three feeding trout. Two were nosing cress bugs in the weed and the third was surface-feeding, probably on ants. It appeared as though the morning held promise for the Ohio boys.

I made my way upstream toward the now-famous S Bend, which has since been removed to make way for Interstate 81. In those days it held a better-than-average number of trout for its length, and there were several respectable browns that called it home. By the time I reached the upper end I'd spotted a total of eight working trout.

At this point I was less than a hundred feet from what was at that time the largest hole on the Letort. Into it, from a springhouse close by, ran the most beautiful little lime-stone springlet I'd ever seen. The water was crystal clear, clean, cold, and a constant fifty to fifty-two degrees. Around three to five feet wide, it was choked with cress for

Terrestrial Fishing

The Jassid (above). A leaf-hopper, inspiration for the Jassid imitation (left).

A —— Selection of Terrestrial Imitations and Naturals

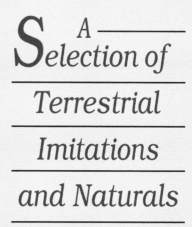

A Letort Japanese Beetle.

A Black Fur Ant.

A Cinnamon Fur Ant.

A McMurray Red Ant.

A McMurray Black Ant.

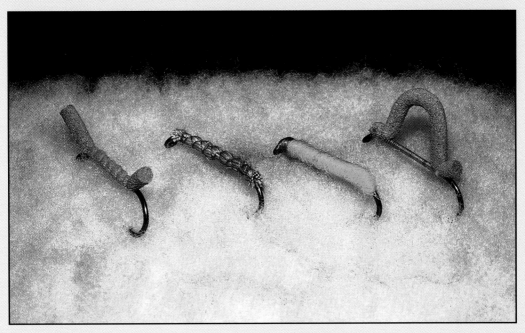

Four inchworm imitations. left to right: Live Body Inchworm; Deer-Hair Inchworm; Yarn Inchworm; Live Body Hump Inchworm.

A grasshopper.

The Letort Hopper.

A brown cricket.

A black cricket.

(Inset) A Letort Cricket.

its entire length. For years Charlie had used it as a nursery for wild brook, and later brown, trout. When I met Charlie in 1957 he had stopped using the little feeder. But the trout had not.

The hole the spring ran into was perhaps ten yards wide and about thirty to forty yards long. At the head of the pool was a formidable brush pile. On a major river it would have been considered a logjam, but here it was perfect big-trout habitat. Below the brush pile a broad flat provided an almost-perfect feeding field for a dozen or more trout. Four deep channels were cut in the weed and each seemed to have its own resident trout population. The shallows between the channels held a good number of year-old brookies that had provided hours of enjoyment during my first years on the Letort. Ed Shenk had seen what he thought to be a trophy brown in the lower end of the hole, but had never been able to take it. Ed was certain the monster lived under the brush pile and drifted back to the middle or tail-end of the pool to feed. I'd never been able to get a look at this fish, even on the days Ed and I fished together.

I stopped well back from the tail-end of the pool and scanned the water from bank to bank. I spotted several brookies darting back and forth in the shallows, but no browns, even in the deeper channels. I moved a few steps forward to watch the pool more closely. I remember thinking to myself, "If those guys get with it they're in for a fantastic morning's fishing." I turned to look downstream toward the meadow I'd left behind, but there was no sign of my friends.

I turned back to continue scanning the water. The sun was up, brightening the water and increasing my ability to see into it. I moved my head from side to side as I systematically covered the water. But on one swing something clicked in my mind. About midstream something wasn't right—it was out of place, too dark, not normal. I strained to see into the water and was able to make out a large, dark object just beyond midstream and a foot or more beneath the water surface. For several minutes I stared into the dark green water hoping for some movement that would indicate I was looking at a trout. For five minutes I watched and whatever it was didn't move. "Time to move on," I thought. "It has to be a log or something."

But as I gave a backward glance as I got up to move on, the dark shape appeared to move as though drifting back toward the tail of the channel. I blinked, looked away, then back again—it *was* moving. My heart began to pound. Slowly the fish drifted back and up so that, in the tail of the channel, it was only six inches or so below the surface. It was a monster brown, every bit as big as the biggest fish I'd yet come across on the Letort. The big fish stopped at the end of the hole and took up a feeding position just inches below the surface. There was no mistaking now; it was the brown Ed Shenk had spotted in this hole many times before. I was almost shaking as I knelt in the grass, watching. Suddenly the huge jaws tilted upward as the trout inhaled something from the surface. A small dimple emerged as a large ring that broke the placid surface of the pool.

I removed my tiny fly from the hookkeeper and began to strip out line. Was the fly too small? Would the gossamer tipper hold if I were lucky enough to hook this fish? What would it do: dive for the depths of the weed or shoot upstream for the logjam? Had this fish come along a few years later, when I'd had more experience with big trout, I would have been a lot calmer. But at that moment, how it might react was a mystery to me. I tried to settle down and keep observing. The fish rose twice more and showed no sign of moving.

In an instant, I made a decision to change to a larger pattern and a heavier tippet. I thought I'd rather lose the fish to a refusal than to a broken tippet of a fly that pulled out. With shaking hands I tied on a three-foot section of 4X. "Calm down," I told myself. "You have to relax a little." Easy enough to say, damn difficult to do!

I flipped open the compartment lid on my chest fly box for the section that held terrestrial patterns. I looked over the ants, beetles, Jassids, hoppers, inchworms, and crickets. I lingered over the section of #12 and #14 cricket patterns Ed Shenk had first shown me just weeks before. I reached in and picked out one of the crickets, #12. The brown still tailed calmly at the end of the hole.

It seemed to take an eternity to tie that fly on, but I finally managed it. "Okay, settle down," I whispered to myself, stripping line from the reel. The sound of the tiny pawl against the gears sounded like a generator engine. "He's going to spook. Be careful," I keep mumbling. "Check out the current. How is it carrying food to him? Will he move to the right or left? Don't spook him with the leader. Turn the line over high in the air so it will land softly. You may have only one chance."

As I began to false-cast, gradually working out line, my nerves began to settle. With thirty feet of line in the air I let the forward cast go upstream and close to my side of the bank, taking no chances that the big brown would see it. I realized it wasn't long enough as the leader straightened and the cricket landed about dead even with the trout's head, but a good twenty feet to its left. I cast again, adding about six more feet of line. The distance was perfect. I let the line and leader drift back, did a roll pick-up, and began another short series of false-casts. I shot the line high in the air and watched it turn a beautiful loop as it approached the trout. The fly touched gently down two feet ahead of the brown. The current moved the cricket drag-free toward the finning monster. Its head turned slightly as the fly entered its window. The cricket drifted slowly past, untouched.

Now my earlier nervousness returned. "Calm down," I whispered. The second cast was a duplicate of the first. The cricket floated flawlessly and naturally past the trout—nothing.

I stripped in the line, coiling it in the grass by my knees. The fly and tippet looked good. The brown rose again, then again.

"Okay, Ed," I said aloud, "Try placing the line and leader on his far side. Throw a left curve and try to drop the fly so it will come straight on into him. Lefty Kreh could do this with one try, but I'm no Lefty." As I think back on that morning, I'm awfully glad no one was there to hear me say these things to myself. They would have thought I'd lost my mind.

I false-casted again, working out an additional five feet of line to allow for the distance needed for a lefthand curve. The line shot through the air well behind the brown. My wrist turned sharply as the leader loop began to straighten, and the last half of the leader snapped crisply to the left. The cricket landed a good two feet in front of the brown and in a straight line with his nose. "Thank you, Lord," I whispered.

The cricket drifted ten inches and the monster nosed up and waited. After another six inches of drag-free drift the head tilted up some more and a ring appeared. The cricket was gone.

Terrestrial Fishing

I raised the tip of the Flea sharply, letting the line slide through my fingers. I felt the hook bite home and in an instant the brown was taking off upstream through the channel in the weed. He was a good twenty yards from the brush pile. He was heavy and powerful. Applying as much pressure as possible to the line, I quickly turned the rod to the right and down low to the water, putting a curve in the line as it cut through the water. The little bamboo stick was bent for all it was worth. The trout continued to surge toward the brush pile.

Suddenly the power of the surge changed direction and I could feel the tiny straining rod turn the trout downstream. He dove deep in the channel and moved past me, downstream. "Thank you," I muttered as he turned and held downstream about thirty feet below me. All this happened in less than thirty seconds and I was still on my knees. Finally, I stood up. I was feeling better about the situation. At least now I could move with the trout and give the advantage to the little rod.

The fish moved up and down the channel at least six times, never reaching the safety of the brush pile. I managed to control it for almost twenty minutes. Each run was less intense than the one before and I was able to move the trout closer to the surface each time. If only the hook would hold!

One more time the fish surged upstream, only on this run it was closer to the surface than it had been. As it raced past me I turned the rod sharply to my left and began reeling like heck while I was still on the bank. There was almost twenty feet of weed just inches below the water's surface between me and the brown. Weed began to tear off and hang on the line, the leader, and the trout. I couldn't move it.

I decided to wade in. My first step off the bank put me in over my waist and I sank helplessly in the mud up to my knees. Movement was impossible. Slowly, cautiously, I eased the trout through the weed, fearing every foot of the way that the weight of the brown plus the weed would snap the leader. I finally could get close enough by leaning over, while water filled my waders, and slide my net under the fish. But because the ball of weed on the leader and fish was so big, it wouldn't fit into the net. In desperation I slid the net under trout, weed, and all, grabbed the package with both hands, and heaved rod, net, trout, and weed onto the bank. I had a devil of a time getting myself out of the river. When I finally made it, I clipped the leader to leave the cricket in the trout's mouth and headed downstream to my friends' tent.

Such carrying on you've never heard. I thought *I* was excited, but not, it turned out, as much as the boys from Ohio. They paraded me to Charlie's meadow, took pictures, shook my hand, slapped me on the back, and made me tell the story again and again. To this day I can't remember all that took place, but I do remember thinking that I finally had my big trout. I'll never forget Charlie saying, "Ed boy, that's a trout of a lifetime."

I sent a picture, the weight and dimensions (9 pounds, 27 1/2 inches), and scale samples of the brown to the Pennsylvania Fish Commission. While the trout was being mounted by a taxidermist I received word from the Commission that the trout was a nine-year-old female and the new Pennsylvania record for a brown trout taken on a dry fly. And although it all happened some twenty-six years ago, it seems like only yesterday to me. I hope it always will.

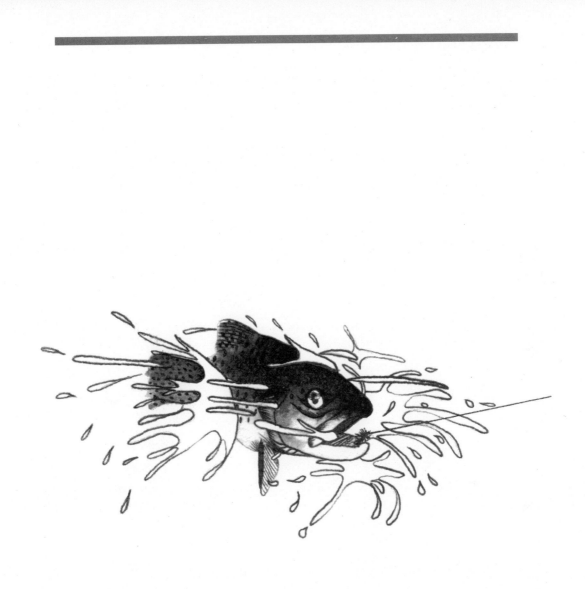

Tackle

8

What follows is a very personal, somewhat idiosyncratic, discussion. To try to compare and make recommendations on the hundreds of rods, reels, lines, fly boxes, waders, vests, and other equipment available would require a separate book. I would rather try to relate my own logic for using the tackle I do. If you are an established fly fisher it may not mean much, but it might. If you are just getting started you may find it helpful.

Prior to my moving to Carlisle in the late 1950s I was stationed at the Marine base in Quantico, Virginia. While there, I found what I thought was my dream rod, the one that would last me the rest of my life. It was a 7 1/2-foot green fiberglass rod by Heddon. I'd never seen a 7 1/2-foot rod before. The cost was $14.50 if memory serves. I purchased the rod and a new Cortland HDH line. To my amazement the clerk provided me with a rod bag and a cardboard rod tube. During the short ride back to the base I was like a kid at Christmas, stroking the rod tube, fantasizing just how the little wand would perform. Minutes after arriving home the new line was on my old 1492 Medalist. I spent the best part of the next hour casting on the lawn with the little rod. It performed even better than I expected. For three years in Virginia and four more in Pennsylvania it was the only rod I used.

When I started my tackle shop in Carlisle in 1959, I became a Shakespeare dealer. My next rod was a Shakespeare 6 1/2-footer. Somewhat sadly, I replaced my little Heddon with it. Several years later a good friend began representing Fenwick rods and I acquired a 6-foot Beauty and a 7-foot Fenwick for bigger work. Next came bamboo from Sewall Dunton and, later, Orvis. Then came graphite and a trio of Orvis 6 1/2-foot Fleas: one for my son, one for my wife, and one for me. Next came three seven-foot nine-inchers. Some years later along came a Loomis 7-foot for a three-weight, an 8-foot for a four-weight, and an 8 1/2-foot for a six-weight. The final rod was a Fenwick Boron/Graphite 9-foot for a five-weight. Don't bother to add them up. They come to too many! My den is sixteen by twenty-two and I'm having a tough time finding room to store and display twenty-five years of rod accumulation. Today I use two of those rods ninety percent of the time.

A good single-action reel is, in my opinion, the next priority for someone just getting started. The Pflueger is perhaps the most serviceable and least expensive. I think Orvis's new reels are great. The reels I use today are more than twenty years old. I own several Hardy Featherweights and Lightweights, and Orvis CFO II's and III's. They have seen hundreds of hours of hard use and are as good today as they were the day I purchased them.

For a beginner, I would recommend a weight-forward fly line. It will make casting easier for someone just starting.

For dry-fly and midge fishing, I prefer a double taper. In moderate casting ranges it makes delicate deliveries a breeze. An added bonus with the double taper is that you can use both ends, doubling the life of the line.

More years ago than I care to remember, Lee Wulff designed a new fly line that was marketed by Garcia. It was fantastic and I used it for as many years as it was available. It was called a Long Belly Torpedo Taper. Unfortunately, Garcia discontinued it some years ago. If you ever find a dust-covered example on a shelf in some remote tackle shop, buy it. Lee believed enough in the concept (thank goodness) that several years ago he produced another unique fly line, the Lee Wulff Triangle Taper. It is a slightly different taper with even greater casting capability than the original Long Belly. For delicate, light work, standard casting, or heavy-duty work, it can't be beat. I now use a 2/3 and a 4/5 almost exclusively.

Since the early 1960s, I have used knotted leaders. The first knotted leaders I ever encountered were tied by Art Newman of the Wanigas Rod Company in Saginaw, Michigan. (Saginaw is Wanigas spelled backward, or is it the other way around?) I can't recall the circumstances of that first meeting with Art, but I will be forever indebted to him for his leader formula. I have used it for twenty-five-plus years now.

Knotted leaders will turn over and deliver a fly more consistently than will the knotless type. If a tippet is snapped off, a knotted leader replacement is quite simple. A custom-tied leader should last an entire season if the last three sections are replaced periodically. The knotted leaders also float better than the knotless type do.

In the 1950s and 1960s most of my leaders were 7 1/2 feet or 9 feet. Today I use 10-foot 5X or 6X and 12-foot 6X lengths. At times I will lengthen the 12-foot leaders to 14 or 16 feet for late-season terrestrial or midge fishing. If you need to fish finer or longer all you have to do with the custom-tied leader is cut back the tippet section and add 6X, 7X, or 8X sections.

Here's the formula for my 10-foot and 12-foot leaders:

LEADER FORMULAS

10-foot, 6X	12-foot, 7X
48" .019	54" .021
18" .015	24" .017
12" .013	12" .013
6" .011	10" .011
6" .009	8" .009
6" .007	6" .007
24" .005	6" .005
	24" .003

Over the years I have spent a lot of money on waders and hip boots, all of it out of necessity because they leaked. I doubt I ever got three years use out of a pair of waders or hippers. Five years ago I decided to try the relatively new lightweight nylon stocking-foot type, and I have yet to patch them. I use both the stocking-foot hippers and waders. They have given me excellent service. The really great thing about them is that they cost half as much as boot-foot hippers and waders.

I have used trout nets since I was a teenager and I still advocate their use. There are many pros and cons over net use, but I think the pros outweigh the cons. A trout brought to net without being entirely fatigued usually flops and thrashes about and sometimes the gills become entangled in the net cord. Damage to the trout can be serious when this happens if care is not taken with release. On the other hand, I have seen inexperienced anglers who did not use a net grasp fish and squeeze so hard in order to remove the fly that I would venture to guess more than fifty percent of these trout did not survive.

For years I've used a little trick with my standard-size net bag to eliminate this problem. I wrap a stout rubber band on the handle of the net. The bottom of the bag is pulled under the rubber band. The result is a flat, tight surface along the net frame. This keeps the bag from catching on the brush when I walk the banks. Also, trout when brought to net just lie on top of the net frame rather than down in the bag, eliminating the danger of gills becoming tangled in the bag.

About eight years ago my wife was cleaning out her sewing room. The pile of discards was rather large, so she asked me to put them in a trash bag and take it out for her. Now I'm rather a frugal fellow and anything I think may be useful next week, next month, or next year usually gets stashed somewhere. While depositing the sewing remnants in the trash bag, I came upon a rather large piece of beautiful nylon-mesh netting. The material intrigued me for a couple reasons: one, it was nylon; and two, the holes were only about the size of a pencil eraser. The following weekend I fashioned a net bag from the new material and strung it on my favorite frame. It has been the most safe and trouble-free net I have ever used. Why some manufacturer hasn't discovered and used this material I don't know.

Limestoners & Freestoners

9

Before I moved to Carlisle, Pennsylvania, in 1957, all of my fishing was done on freestone streams in the central and north-central regions of the state. My first venture to the Letort in Carlisle was a real shock. I was accustomed to fast-flowing freestone mountain streams, and this slow-flowing placid-surfaced murky-colored stream appeared to be anything but trout water. It flowed through farm meadows with six-foot-high weeds on both banks and no rocks or gravel on the bottom. Weeds choked the river bottom and there were only a few deep channels that might perhaps offer cover for trout. I was disappointed, to put it mildly. This couldn't be the water with its mayfly hatches and wild brown trout that Charlie Fox wrote of so enthusiastically. I walked the entire length of the river hoping beyond hope that I would find a least one stretch that resembled what I thought of as trout water, but I didn't. Never even assembling my gear, I just wandered up and down the river in disbelief. In later years I was able to empathize with anglers who visited my shop mumbling that this really couldn't be the famous Letort! On my first trip I felt just as they did.

A friend who attended the same church I did in Carlisle offered to meet me on the Letort one evening for some sulfur fishing and I jumped at the chance. Several evenings later I met him at the quarry on the upper end of the river. I was apprehensive about the evening. As we readied our gear Duke told me that the hatch had been on for a week or more and that he expected a good spinner fall that evening. It was about the third week of May as I recall. As we headed downstream Duke pointed out areas that held substantial numbers of trout. He spotted several trout up and feeding. We stopped and watched for a few minutes.

"Remember where they are," he said. "We'll hit them as we fish back upstream."

I was ready to hit them right then. There really were trout here. I felt relieved. Anticipation grew and I looked forward to the evening's fishing.

A little farther downstream Duke stopped again at a long, flat, quiet glide. It was one of the few sections of the stream with an abundance of trees and the limbs hung out over the water fifteen or twenty feet up from both banks to cover the water. There were trout working regularly there.

"Put on a size fourteen dun," Duke advised, "and wait a few minutes before you start to fish. You stay here and I'll go to the open area just below the trees and start. Unless we catch or put these trout down, we should be able to spend the evening here."

I did as he suggested, finding an area with sufficient casting room. I knelt in the grass along the bank and watched. The trout were all within thirty feet of me. I began to feel better and better.

Terrestrial Fishing

Downstream, Duke had been working on his first trout. I watched as he cast. He had no more than twenty feet of line out and he was below the trout quartering upstream. His tiny sulfur touched the water delicately and began to drift toward the rising trout. I saw his rod lift abruptly and heard him yell "Got him." Shortly the trout was brought to net, Duke removed the fly, held the brown for me to see, and gently eased it back into the water. "About twelve or thirteen inches," he exclaimed.

Now I really began to feel better about this unusual limestone stream. Upstream about twenty yards, at the head of the pool I was watching, two more trout began to feed. Unable to contain myself any longer, I went to work on the trout nearest me. After the third cast it stopped feeding; I'd put it down. I reeled in and watched. The remaining trout continued to feed. Working out line, I dropped the fly to the left of the closest trout. It drifted past where I'd seen the last ring on the water and—nothing. I made several more casts and nothing. It didn't rise again. I'd put down two for two. "You're too anxious and a little nervous," I thought to myself as I reeled in and watched the remaining trout. The flies were more abundant by now and the interval between rises was shorter. Slowly, I worked my way a few feet up the bank to a better casting position for trout number three. Working out line, I carefully placed the little sulfur just a few feet above the fish's last ring. Gently the fly drifted by, but nothing happened. Four casts later, and nothing. I'd put down three in a row. In the meantime Duke had hooked and released two more trout.

Trout number four continued to feed close to the far bank. I watched for a while as he fed and tried to figure out what I was doing wrong. Finally working up enough courage (but not confidence, I had none left), I prepared to cast.

Working out line, I dropped the fly a good two feet ahead of where I'd last seen the trout's ring. The fly drifted toward the brown and a small, delicate dimple appeared in the surface film. I jerked the rod back abruptly, and again nothing. I'd missed number four. Some forty five minutes had passed and I had not touched a single trout.

At the head of the pool another trout had begun to feed. I worked my way upstream and watched. By now the flies were heavy and more trout were working. Stripping out line again, I dropped the sulfur close to the nearest trout. It hadn't drifted a foot when a delicate dimple broke the surface and the fly disappeared. I struck and felt the hook bite home. The trout took off upstream, peeling line from the reel. It charged straight through the head of the pool and on upstream. The trout felt strong and its surging vibrations transferred from leader to line to rod. Now all I hoped for was that I wouldn't lose it. Slowly it began to give way to the pressure of the little 7 1/2-foot rod. It was now in the head of the original pool. Several minutes later a beautiful heavy brown of about twelve inches was in my net. I removed the fly and held the fish in the water for a few minutes, admiring the brilliant colors and stout body. It was very different from the stocked trout I'd been accustomed to. "So this is a wild Letort brown trout," I thought to myself as I looked upstream for another rise. The trout had bolted through the head of the pool and the two remaining fish were no longer feeding. I turned and walked downstream to meet Duke. He had landed and released five trout and missed several others. Though I'd only hooked one fish, it had been a fantastic evening for me. At least now I knew that the stories I'd heard about this stream were true.

The limestone streams in the Cumberland Valley, the Letort, Big Spring, Green Spring, Yellow Breeches, and

Falling Spring, were different from anything to which I had been exposed. They start deep in the limestone strata of the valley and may run underground for miles before coming to the surface. The average water temperature where these springs emerge is usually a constant fifty to fifty-two degrees. The volume of water can vary from several hundred gallons per minute to several thousands of gallons per minute, as is the case with Big Spring and the Boiling Springs, which feeds the Yellow Breeches. Big Spring, near Newville, is reportedly one of the three largest limestone springs in the eastern United States. Though limestone springs run primarily through meadow lands for most of their entire lengths, their year-round water temperatures remain much cooler than any freestone waters in the area. Their gradient drop is no more than fifty feet to one hundred feet from their source to the point at which they enter a major stream or river. This is a distance of perhaps seven miles for Green Spring to thirty-seven miles for the Yellow Breeches. So, their rate of flow is considered slow as compared to faster-falling freestone streams. The streambed is made up of sandy gravel and silt. This condition is ideal for the growth of weeds, cress, and elodea and limestoners are usually weed-choked from bank to bank. There is a benefit to this because the channels formed in the weed beds provide excellent cover and various aquatic life benefits from the growth. A handful of cress or elodea lifted from the water will reveal cress bugs, freshwater shrimp, and mayfly nymphs. The trout-holding capacity of these streams is rated at several thousand pounds of fish per acre of water. Few freestone streams in the East can make this claim. I sometimes wonder why trout ever surface to feed with so much underwater food available. But I'm thankful that they do.

These special stream conditions require special angling techniques. With slow-moving currents the trout don't have to expend the energy to feed that their freestone counterparts do. Limestone trout can take up a feeding position and feed at their leisure as long as they are not disturbed by angler or predator. The slow currents enable the trout to inspect their prey far more closely than freestone trout can. This is a great advantage for the trout, but disaster for the angler. The placid surface of the limestoners requires a flawless presentation every time. A sloppy cast, dragging fly, or leader crossing the trout's window will send it scurrying for cover. Fishing the water on freestoners can be very productive but on limestoners it works for only a talented few. Ed Shenk is one of those few. He knows the water and knows where the trout hold and feed. He locates trout throughout the season and always works the water just as though he were working a rising trout. It sounds simple, but believe me, it is not. It took me years, and I do mean *years*, to be able to read and fish the water half as well as Ed does.

In the early days I would sit in the meadow with Charlie when things were slow, and he would talk by the hour about the years of trial-and-error trying to get the upper hand with the Letort browns. Charlie, Vince, Ed Shenk, and other regulars had had more than fifteen years on this water before I met them in 1957. Charlie's conclusion was to fish only to working trout, that is, trout that are feeding beneath the surface that could be seen, and of course surface feeders. He felt that pounding the water trying to drum up trout was a waste of time. He played then, and does now, a waiting game. When he finds a feeding trout, he goes to work on him. His success rate is phenomenal. There are times he doesn't take a feeding trout, but it isn't often.

The most frustrating thing for me on this new water was learning to get a drag-free float. My casting was respectable and I could cast a long line if necessary. Accuracy wasn't a problem; I could place a fly within six inches of my feeding fish. But the minute the fly touched the water it immediately began to drag. No matter what I did or how I tried, I couldn't overcome the problem. I finally admitted it was time for another chat with Charlie.

I met Charlie at the bench in his meadow and at great length poured out my problem. I was really frustrated and Charlie knew it. "Yes," he started, "we had the same problem and it took us the best part of a season to figure it out." I knew he had the solution, and I was relieved. "The currents are devilish hard here," he continued. "The stream is perhaps thirty to forty feet wide on average. Some sections may reach sixty to seventy feet in width. Looking at the slow-moving, apparently undisturbed surface is deceiving. You think a perfectly straight line cast will produce a perfect drift for your fly, but it doesn't. There may be only two or as many as six varying currents that are imperceptible to a new angler. These currents are formed by the thick growth of the weed beds. As the weed reaches full growth and nears the water surface, the current will form channels from a foot to as much as four feet wide in the weed. The water moving over and through these channels is moving three or four times faster than the water flowing over only a few inches of weed near the surface. The speed of the channel water causes the drag problem. When a cast is made, if the fly drags immediately on landing on the water, your leader has crossed a channel in the weed. If that happens, let the float continue and watch the fly line. If more bellies form in the line, it is over additional current channels in the weed. Make a mental note of the number of bellies that show up in the leader and fly line. It may only be one, but it may be three or four in a thirty foot cast. This is the problem you have to eliminate."

"How?"

"Easily! You throw S curves in your line and leader."

I thanked Charlie for his help and advice and told him I would head upstream, try to find some feeding trout, and give his technique a try. What I really had in mind was to get out of Charlie's sight so he wouldn't see how bad my casting might be. I was intimidated by this water and felt very insecure about my abilities in those years. It took a few seasons to master the techniques for this new water, but eventually my trout-taking success ratio began to improve.

For a period of twelve years or more I fished almost exclusively on the limestone water of the Cumberland Valley. I doubt that I made a dozen trips in that time to fish freestone waters. The challenge and intrigue of the limestoners can keep one busy for a lifetime. In the 1950s and early 1960s the streams were never crowded. But as articles and books were written and news was spread by word of mouth about this angling Mecca, fly fishermen from all over the country converged on the Cumberland Valley. By 1967, most regulars never ventured to the water on weekends, knowing it would be difficult, if not impossible, to find fishing room. The development of the terrestrial patterns opened the door to an extended season of trout fishing for thousands of eastern anglers within several hours drive of the Cumberland Valley. Thus, fishing pressure on the weekends eventually drove the locals and regulars to seek alternative weekend fishing.

Until this time the terrestrial patterns were used exclusively on limestone waters. I doubt that any of the locals ever considered trying them anywhere else. Any of us, that is, save Ed Shenk. He had been using them on some of his favorite freestone streams for years and they were just as effective.

One of my earliest excursions out of the Cumberland Valley was to Potter County in the north-central part of Pennsylvania. I had a ball fishing the feeder streams of Big Pine Creek with ants, hoppers, crickets, and beetles. Thirty or forty trout taken in a morning's fishing was normal. I was astounded and pleasantly so. For the next several seasons I began fishing many of the freestoners bordering Cumberland County. The terrestrial patterns were just as effective there as they were on the Letort, Big Spring, or Falling Spring.

Some years later I spent a week in Vermont with Tony Skilton in early August. We fished a half dozen or so of Tony's favorite secret streams with terrestrials and took more trout than I had ever hooked on the Letort. Another good friend, Bruce Parker, lives in Mountain City, Tennessee. He told me that from mid-July on he can take trout at will on hoppers, crickets, and ants.

One of the early fly shops to which I sold terrestrial patterns was Bud Lilly's in West Yellowstone, Montana. He purchased as many hoppers, crickets, and ants as Orvis did in those days, the only difference being that Bud ordered larger sizes. I found out why on a trip to West Yellowstone in 1972. The flies were bigger, the fish were bigger, the rivers were bigger, and the country was bigger. Everything was bigger in Montana.

Although the terrestrials were not developed or intended for freestone waters, they have certainly added a new dimension to late-summer and early-fall fishing for anglers everywhere. But obviously, terrestrial fishing presents a rather dramatic change in techniques compared to early-season tactics. Numerous factors, from river conditions to tackle and approach, make this challenging but effective approach to mid- and late-season angling worth trying.

On the limestone streams in the Cumberland Valley during the early half of the season the weed, cress, and elodea have not reached full growth. This makes the water flow appear to be less than we are normally used to seeing it. The water appears lower and much cover that will hold trout in the late summer and early fall is exposed. As the aquatic growth matures, it raises the water level and oftentimes pushes the water over the banks and into the meadows. It is something like dumping tons of rock in the river or building a twelve-inch-high dam from bank to bank. By July, this phenomenon has increased trout holding and feeding habitat by some forty to sixty percent. The river will stay that way until the following spring when the weed dies off or is washed out (*purged* as the locals refer to it) with the high water of spring. What this means to the angler is that the limestoners do not reach their prime until mid-season. Instead of declining as fishable water, as happens with freestone streams in late summer, by that time the limestoners are just getting good. The water stays cold because of the deep spring origins, and the meadows through which it meanders are rich with insect life: ants, beetles, hoppers, crickets, inchworms, and caterpillars. There is no dwindling food supply for the fish in these waters during late summer and early fall. So you see how the development of terrestrial patterns extended our season here by four or five months.

Limestoners in the East are usually fished from the banks. This more often than not creates difficult casting situations. Weeds are usually waist-high along the banks, requiring high backcasts. First-time visitors to our waters usually drive home mumbling and muttering about the damnable weeds.

Wading is kept to a minimum for a number of reasons. When the water spreads and reaches out over the banks, perhaps as much as two to six feet, footing becomes treacherous. An angler not knowing the river can sink knee-deep in mud with one wrong step. It is almost impossible to wade across these streams because of the soft silted bottoms, and wading will send a trail of muddy water downstream, making it difficult or impossible for downstream anglers to have fishable water.

Freestone streams, on the other hand, experience conditions just the reverse. Their water levels fall to perhaps thirty to fifty percent of normal after April or May. They are reduced to trickling riffles and quiet, slow-moving pools. Their water temperatures may reach into the seventies and sometimes eighties. These are difficult conditions for insects, trout, and anglers. Their only saving grace is that springs and small feeder streams hold up during the hot, late months of summer.

In late summer the major hatches are over. Terrestrials, caddis, and midges now become the fare of the day. Some may not find this kind of fishing as pleasing esthetically as that in the early season, but it can be as much fun. Advantages swing to the angler's side during this time of year. Wading is easier and trout can be seen more readily. Long, fine leaders help overcome the low, clear water conditions.

The approach to limestone or freestone streams during the late season has to be quiet, slow, cautious, and observant. During the late season I usually pick a section of stream to fish and walk downstream a quarter- to a half-mile, figuring I will fish about twice that distance when I've finished. As I walk downstream, I stay well back from the river, oftentimes ten yards or more, to avoid spooking or putting down trout. I walk slowly and quietly, as though stalking squirrel or deer. It's amazing how many trout a heavy-footed angler puts down without ever realizing it. As I move downstream I first look for rising trout. Next, I look for trout in feeding positions. Often I will locate a minimum of a dozen and as many as thirty or forty trout on my trek downstream. I mark each trout's location mentally, then work each on the way upstream. Knowing where to look for fish eliminates the chance I'll spook them carelessly.

I never assemble my rod until I've reached my starting point. I check the water carefully as I rig up my gear. More often than not, before I've tied on my fly I've located several fish on which to work.

On limestoners I usually crouch or get on my knees to work into casting position. On freestoners I'll locate a spot with casting room and work my way to it, whether I'm on the bank or wading in the stream. If you use a cautious approach and locate trout on a preliminary downstream trip, you will increase your success potential by at least thirty percent. You will know where the trout are and you will not spook them as you work your way upstream because you will be expecting them in a given location.

As I mentioned earlier, often I locate one, two, or more trout in the area I've selected to start fishing. By the time I've worked over those trout I've usually found several more to work as I slowly and quietly move upstream. The process repeats itself over and over again: work the trout, locate other trout, move upstream, repeat the process. Seldom if ever do I find it necessary to fish the water. The ability to see fish is the first ingredient for successful late-season trouting.

Ed Shenk taught me to see trout some thirty years ago. In

this regard he is uncanny. On freestone or limestone he could pick out trout twenty, thirty, forty, and even sixty feet away as easily as I could see a cow in a pasture. It took several seasons, but I finally learned how to see trout. More than anything else, the ability to see the fish has increased my trout-taking abilities.

It is easier to see trout in freestone streams during the late season when the water is low and gin-clear. The trout stand out vividly against the brown-colored sand, gravel, and stones. The darker color of the trout's back and sides make them easy to spot. On the limestoners it's different because the weed in the streams is dark green and the trout's colors blend in with the background of the stream bottom. I strongly recommend learning to see trout on freestoners first. Once you can accomplish this easily on freestone water, the transition to using the technique on limestone waters will not be as difficult.

The most effective approach for a beginner is to walk to the tail of a well-lighted pool on your favorite freestone stream. Stand back from the bank using brush or trees behind you as cover. Polaroids are a necessity. Use gray or tan; it doesn't matter. Scan the water from the tail to the head of the pool for a rising trout. If you see a trout rise, causing the familiar ring on the water's surface, the battle is half over. Now look *into* the water where the ring appeared—not just at the surface. Most anglers observe miles of surface water during the course of a season and never see anything that takes place an inch or more beneath it. As you look at the ring of a.rising trout, look into the water at that point until the detail of the stream bottom becomes clear. Gravel, stones, logs, whatever, will begin to materialize. Continue to watch the stream bottom. Now look for movement: a tail gently swaying, fins moving, or a head moving left or right, up or down. If you are really looking *into* the water and can see the tan or brown-colored bottom, any movement, no matter how slight, will stand out. If you see something dark move in contrast to the lighter color of the stream, ninety percent of the time it will be a trout.

Once you've found a trout beneath the surface, watch it for several minutes or longer. Is it holding in position watching for insects floating on the surface? Is it moving from right to left, up or down, forward or backward, looking for drifting insects beneath the surface? Its movements will indicate what type of artificial you should use. After observing for a while, look away, then look back again until you find the trout. Don't be in a hurry; in fact, repeat the looking-away-and-back process several times. The ability to locate and see trout is the first and most important technique in late-season low-water angling success.

The second, and equally as important, technique is the wading approach. Chances are if you have spotted your trout while standing back from the water's edge, you will have to move or perhaps enter the stream to get into an advantageous casting position. If you must enter the water, do so slowly. Whatever your conception of slowly is, immediately cut it in half. As you enter the stream do not lift your foot above the water and put it down as though you were stepping into a bathtub. Slide your foot gently into the water. Make sure the footing in the streambed is solid, and then slide (without lifting) your other foot ahead of you—slowly. If you don't send a flurry of waves out into the stream, you have done it right. As you continue to move, slide your feet slowly without lifting them out of the water. Watch the trout as you move. As long as it continues to feed or continues to hold in feeding position things are going your way. Take your time. The trout is at home; he's not going anywhere unless you spook him. When you feel you've reached a comfortable casting position, go to work. If you learn to master wading still water without spooking trout, eighty percent of your battle is won. Wading in riffles or broken water is a snap compared to placid pools.

A critical aspect of late-season angling is wading noise. Most anglers are unaware of the noise they make as they move about the stream. You can't hear the noise you make, but the trout can. As you wade you dislodge stones and you crush and roll small gravel underfoot. The trout hear this. I've emphasized moving slowly while wading. The slower you move, the more aware you are of loose stones that roll or slide as you put weight on them. If a streambed is mostly small gravel, place your foot down carefully on the stones, allowing the pressure of your foot to slowly increase. This eliminates rubbing or crunching of the stones.

A third technique critical to late-season terrestrial work is casting accuracy. Being able to see trout and wade quietly is great, but not worth a tinker's darn if you can't present your fly properly and accurately. I've preached casting accuracy for years to friends, customers, students, and clients. Some have taken the advice and gone on to become proficient anglers, others are still struggling and frustrated, just as they were twenty years ago. Perhaps the advice seems too simple to take to heart. But for what it's worth, I'll describe it again.

In your backyard, lawn, or wherever, take a paper plate eight to ten inches in diameter and place it on the grass. Now, step off twenty paces from the plate. Start casting at the paper target, trying to place the leader on the plate with every cast. It may take five minutes or a half-hour or several evenings, but if you stick with it long enough you will be able to hit the target ninety percent of the time. When you can do it consistently at twenty feet, move back to thirty feet. When you can do it at thirty feet, move back to forty feet. When you can hit the plate accurately at forty feet almost every time, you will have accomplished an important goal. Accurate casting will have become second nature and you won't even have to think about what you are doing. I know it sounds overly simple—and it is. But it *does* work. If you are serious about your fly fishing, give it a try.

10

Charles K. Fox

His Influence

In July of 1957 I moved to the Carlisle area in south-central Pennsylvania. Recently discharged from the Marine Corps, I had taken a position with the state as a data processing supervisor. Within a month or so my copy of *Outdoor Life* arrived and in it was Joe Brooks's article on the Jassid. I was astonished to read about the Jassid and its development, the Letort, and Charlie Fox, all of Carlisle. Although I was born and raised about seventy-five miles north of that area, I'd never even heard of or been to the Cumberland Valley. I figured, once I was there, that I would have to drive hours to find any good trout fishing. Perusing the article for the third time (in the same evening), my excitement built with every word as Joe explained in detail the Jassid's development, the spring run and its wild trout, the abundant mayfly hatches, and the free-rising trout.

I determined to find this Letort. I thought I might even be lucky enough one day to happen on Charlie Fox as he fished. I might have the courage to introduce myself, strike up a conversation, and glean information firsthand from this famous fellow. These and other wild thoughts raced through my mind. Work for the next week became difficult. By the beginning of the second week I knew I would turn into a basket case if I wasn't able (and soon) to satisfy my desire. I managed to find out where Charlie lived and even drove by the lane that led to his home. I drove to several parking areas along the stream and walked down to look at the water. I was making progress. I kept rehearsing over and over again in my mind what I would say when and if I finally got to meet him.

One evening during the middle of the week, when I was certain Charlie's dinner would be over, I drove across town, parked in front of the white house, mustered up some courage, walked up, and knocked on the door. My thoughts were racing and my heart was beating even faster. I just knew I would become tongue-tied the minute the door opened, no matter who answered. The palms of my hands began to sweat profusely. Suddenly the door opened and there he stood, easily recognizable from the pictures in *Outdoor Life*. "Charlie Fox?" I blurted, thankful the words came out right.

"Yes, can I help you?" he replied softly.

"Yes, I'm Ed Koch. I just moved here last month. I read Joe Brooks's article in *Outdoor Life* about the Jassid. Wonder if I could talk to you about it and wonder if you could show me a fly. It doesn't have to be now if you're busy. I can come back another time. I know I should have called first, but I was driving by and decided to stop. I'm a fly fisherman and sort of fly tier." I rambled on without batting an eye or taking a breath. I was sure Charlie must have thought I was some kind of nut.

"No, it's alright, come on in." I thought I heard him say it as I stood there unable to move, as though my feet were cemented into the concrete of his porch. "Come on in, dinner is finished and I've got some time. Be glad to talk with you," he answered a second time standing there holding the front door open. By the time I snapped back to reality I was standing in the center of the most awe-inspiring living room I had ever seen: knotty pine paneled walls, hardwood floors, huge fireplace, cathedral ceiling, beautiful paintings on the walls, many by Fred Everett. Several bamboo rods were at the ready next to the fireplace. It was the kind of room I had read about in *Outdoor Life*.

I sat down on the sofa next to Charlie. On the long coffee table there was an assortment of fly-fishing paraphernalia: several boxes of flies, coiled leaders, leather fly wallets, a reel, a copy of *Outdoor Life* with Joe's article. Charlie picked up one of the small plastic boxes and dumped its contents on the table. There were a dozen of the most beautiful, delicate flies I'd ever seen—the new Jassid. I was mesmerized. The tiny gold-and-white jungle-cock eyes seemed to sparkle in the artificial light of Charlie's living room. The tiny flies were tied with various hackle colors: black, brown, grizzly, cream, and olive. He placed several in the palm of his hand, holding them closer for my observation, as he described the reason for the unique design. They had to float flat in the surface film, not stand upright upon it, as with the standard dry fly. He told me every intricate detail of the discovery, development, and angling technique as though he were passing on words of wisdom to a son. We talked. No—I asked questions, Charlie talked, and in the wink of an eye four hours passed. I could have sat and listened all night and though I didn't realize it then, Charlie could have talked for hours on end of forty years in pursuit of trout. I apologized, excused myself, thanked him, invited myself back again, thanked him, excused myself, thanked him again, all in one breath. "Come back anytime," I heard him say as I was halfway out the door.

That was my introduction to Charlie Fox in 1957. In my mind it is as though it were yesterday. I don't remember the drive home because I was on cloud nine. Little did I realize how that night would change and influence my life. It was only the beginning.

For a period of seven years I took advantage of every opportunity to spend time with Charlie, sometimes fishing the Letort, other times sitting on one of the benches in his meadow listening to the experiences of thirty years of fishing. These were wonderful times for me. I'd been an ardent fly fisher from the age of twelve, but these encounters with Charlie launched a thirty-year apprenticeship.

Once a week Charlie had lunch with a group of anglers who worked in or around Harrisburg. He invited me to join them. There I met Vince Marinaro, Frank Metzger, Charlie Knier, Jim Kell, Bruce Brubaker (a former world casting champion), Ross Trimmer, Joe Carricato, and occasional out-of-towners who, when in Harrisburg on business, would join the group. This group, I learned, was the backbone of the Fly Fishers Club of Harrisburg, a decidedly non-organized group who held their 42nd annual dinner in 1989. Discussions at these lunches were always of fishing trips, new water, reports on regularly fished streams, exchanges of fly patterns, information about new hatches, new tackle, new books, and always the concerns with present-day problems and what could be done for the future.

In early 1959, during one of our discussions, I expressed an interest in trying to sell some flies for extra income. "Try mail order," Charlie advised, "That's the only way to reach the large number of fly fishers nationwide. I don't think it would be profitable enough just to try to sell locally. All it would take is a little flyer with some flies described and an advertisement in the classified section of *Outdoor Life*, *Sports Afield*, or *Field & Stream*. Wouldn't cost much to get started." That was all I needed to hear. Sixty days later I had a short ad in the *Outdoor Life* classified section. A week after that issue arrived I began getting requests for brochures. I couldn't believe it was all really happening. Several weeks later the first orders arrived. Over the fall and winter months requests for brochures continued, as did the orders for flies. Every order of flies I mailed out contained a personal note about the flies and how to fish them. During the weekly luncheons, I excitedly kept Charlie up to date on how my little business was progressing, and each week he continued his encouragement. I searched for ways to repay him for his advice, interest, and encouragement and he always replied, "That's okay. I'm glad I could help. Happy things are going well for you." That's the kind of person Charlie is, as I was to discover time and time again over the years.

It was in 1960 or 1961 that I received several letters from customers in the Boston area encouraging me to exhibit at the Boston Sports and Outdoor Show. These people were all members of the fledgling United Fly Tyers and mentioned they could arrange a booth for me next to theirs. They would encourage potential fly tyers and I would sell materials. By that time I'd grown from the original brochure with only a few flies to a small catalog of flies, fly-tying materials, and fly-fishing tackle. I called Charlie, explained the proposal, and arranged a meeting to discuss it with him. When I met him several evenings later he was as excited, if not more, than I was at the possibilities the invitation provided and, as always, he was positive. "Ed, this is a great opportunity for your business as well as for the Letort and the Carlisle area. You will be exposed to thousands of people up there in a week. You can let them know just what we have here as far as trout fishing is concerned. I'll bet that next season we'll see dozens more anglers bring their families or groups of other fly fishers down to sample what the Cumberland Valley has to offer. Get yourself a booth to display your wares, load it up, take extras along, get brochures from our Chamber of Commerce on things to do or see in the area. Show them there is plenty for a family to do and see, and they will come. This is a wonderful opportunity you have, so make the most of it."

It was settled—I was off to Boston. The following day I stopped at the Chamber of Commerce to pick up brochures promoting the Carlisle area. But when I read over the brochures later, I found no mention of trout, fishing, or the Letort. I called Charlie and announced angrily, "There's not one word about fishing in this material. What's the matter with these people? Don't they realize what they have here?"

"Well, it doesn't surprise me," Charlie replied. "But I think there's a solution. We can write and print our own brochure. We can do a better job than they would because we can tell our own story just the way we want it to be told. We know it. They don't."

I immediately felt relieved and set about compiling material and arranging to have five thousand brochures printed. With Charlie's help, I arrived in Boston on time and, I thought, well prepared.

But by the evening of the third day, our fishing brochures were gone. I made a panicky phone call back home to Ed Shenk, who was holding down the fort at my little fly shop, The Yellow Breeches Angler. Somehow he and Charlie worked a miracle or two, and in three days I had more brochures.

At last relaxed enough to enjoy the show, I doubled my catalog mailing list and had the time of my life conversing with the likes of Ted Trueblood, Wes Jordan of the Orvis Company, Tap Tapply, and Ted Williams. Because of Charlie's wisdom and encouragement I was able to do well for myself while doing some good as an ambassador of sorts for the Cumberland Valley. Charlie turned out to be quite correct, too, because that summer we saw a retinue of New England fly fishermen testing our south-central Pennsylvania waters. That yearly pilgrimage continues to this day, except now the fly fishers are from all over the United States.

During the early 1960s Charlie began a correspondence with George Griffith of Michigan, the founding father of Trout Unlimited. Charlie believed strongly that the goals and objectives of T.U. could be the vehicle he had been searching for to help bring about change in Pennsylvania's somewhat unenlightened approach to fishing regulations and conservation. He knew then that the preservation of Pennsylvania's riparian habitats lay in stricter environmental control and catch-and-release fishing. Largely through Charlie's dialogues with George Griffith, a Cumberland Valley chapter of T.U. was formed. The first national meeting of Trout Unlimited was held at Allenberry, on the Yellow Breeches.

Also during this extremely important period in the early 1960s, the Yellow Breeches Anglers and Conservation Association (YBACA) was formed, again through Charlie Fox's influence and foresight. The YBACA applied for and received approval from the Pennsylvania Fish Commission to start a cooperative nursery project on a small limestone spring just outside Harrisburg, Pennsylvania. The Fish Commission provided fingerling trout, and the club purchased feed and raised the trout to stock in a designated five-mile area. The club also secured approval to post the first regulated flies-only area on public water in Pennsylvania. This section, again at Allenberry, became a model enabling other Pennsylvania clubs and eventually T.U. itself to follow suit. By the middle 1970s there were fifty-seven regulated fly-fishing areas in Pennsylvania.

The reputation of the Cumberland Valley, its limestone water, wild trout populations, and the lead it was taking in resource conservation spread. The number of visiting anglers increased with each passing season. The Orvis Company established a fly-fishing school, the first outside Vermont, at Allenberry. The school ran successfully for seven years.

What happened next was probably inevitable, and I admit I did not see it coming. But Charlie did, and with his characteristic optimism and energy he welcomed it with open arms. Letters and phone calls in large number began coming in from fly-fishing groups all over the East. "Can you come speak to us?" they asked. "Tell us what you have done and how we can do it, too." "Help us get the message across about catch-and-release fishing and stream conservation."

And soon Charlie, Vince Marinaro, Norm Shires and I, among others, began traveling to speak to these organizations about the fish-for-fun concept, catch-and-release regulations, and the importance of stream habitat conservation. We've all seen the fruit of that labor, particularly in Pennsylvania, as more "flies only" areas are established and more anglers are educated not only in how to catch trout, but how to preserve the resource. And through it all I see the guiding influence of Charlie Fox. In much the same way I am grateful for his friendship and tutelage, fly fishers for years to come can be grateful for his vision and commitment. Thanks, Charlie.

Index

Alaman, Harry, 49-51
Angelo, Frank, 117
Ants
   black, 61, 76-78
   cinnamon, 61, 71-73
   flying ant hatches, 64-66
   Fur body, 68, 79
   hard-back, 59
   McMurray, 81
   Para-, 123
   Rubber Body, 80
   sizes for, 60-61
   tying of, 79-81
   Wet, 59
   white, 63-64

Beck, Barry, 51-52
Beetles
   black, 47, 48
   chumming with live, 36-38
   clipped-deer-hair, 42, 43-45, 47, 49-51, 56
   early use of, 35-36
   "Flure," 39-40
   fly patterns, 39-40, 41-42
   foam-rubber, 39-40, 55
   Grass, 53
   Japanese, 35-41, 54
   importance of size, 47-48
   ladybug, 48
   Live Body, 122
   tying of, 54-57
   Willow, 57
Black ants, 61, 76-78
Brooks, Joe, 20, 101, 105

Casting techniques, 152-53, 157-58
Cinnamon ants, 61, 71-73
Clipped-deer-hair beetles, 42, 43-45, 47, 49-51, 56
Compleat Angler (Walton), 14
Crickets
   development of, 103-4
   size #12, 105, 131-34
   size #14, 113
   size #16, 109, 110, 111,
   success with, 105-14, 131-34

Deer-hair beetles, 42, 43-45, 47, 49-51, 56
Deer-hair Inchworm, 118-19
Dubois, Don, 39-40

Fenwick rods, 138
Finlay, G. Dick, 91
Fisherman's Paradise, 83
Fishing the Midge (Koch), 14
"Flure," 39-40

Fly Fishers Club, 164
Fly-Fisher's Entomology, The
 (Ronalds), 14-15
Flying ant hatches, 64-66
Foam-rubber Beetle, 39-40, 55
Fox, Charles, 12, 13, 19-21, 39, 40-
 41, 84, 85-89, 148-50, 161-169
Freestone waters, fishing in
 approaching, 153-54, 155-57
 casting techniques in, 153, 157-58
 length of season in, 153
 spotting fish in, 155-57
 use of terrestrials in, 151-52
Fur body ants, 60, 79

Gibson, George, 12
Gilson, Jim, 117
Grass Beetle, 53
Griffith, George, 167

Hardy Featherweights and
 Lightweights, 138
Hip boots, 140
Honisch, Frank, 23
Hoppers. *See* Letort hoppers

Inchworm
 Deer-hair, 118-19
 Live Body, 121
 Live Body Hump, 121
 Yarn, 120

Japanese beetles, 35-41, 54
Jassids
 approaching trout with, 22-23
 casting, 22, 24-31
 early use of, 20-22
 tying of, 20, 32-33

Kissinger, Chuck, 62-63
Knotted leaders, 139-40

Leiser, Eric, 31

Letort hoppers
 chumming with live, 88-89
 early patterns, 84
 size #14, 92-96
 Pontoon, 86-88
 success with wing tied flat, 89-91
 tying of, 98-101
 yellow-deer-hair clipped-bodied, 85
Lightner, Norm, 21
Lilly, Bud, 151
Limestone streams, fishing in
 angling techniques for, 148
 approaching, 153-54
 casting techniques in, 152-53, 157-
 58
 description of, 147
 drag-free float in, 149-50
 length of season in, 152
 spotting fish in, 155-57
Lines
 double taper, 139
 Lee Wulff Triangle Taper, 139
 Long Belly Torpedo Taper, 139
 weight-forward fly, 138
Live Body Beetle, 122
Live Body Hump Inchworm, 121
Live Body Inchworm, 121
Loomis rods, 138

McMurray Ant, 81
Marinaro, Vincent, 11, 12, 13, 19-21,
 39, 85, 86-88
Michievicz, Jack, 117
Modern Dry Fly Code, A (Marinaro),
 13, 20

Nets, 140-41
Newman, Art, 139

Orvis, 90-91, 138, 168

Para-ant, 123
Parker, Bruce, 151

Pflueger reel, 138
Phillips Fly Company, 84
Pontoon Hoppers, 86-88

Reels, 138
Rising Trout (Fox), 13
Rods, 137-38
Ronalds, Alfred, 14-15
Rubber Body Ant, 80

Schweibert, Ernest, 12, 88-89
Sewall Dunton, 138
Shakespeare rod, 138
Shenk, Ed, 12, 42, 61, 63, 89-90,
    102-5, 148
Shires, Norm, 73-74, 76-78, 109-14
Skilton, Tony, 66-69, 91-96
Slaymaker, Sam, 12

Tackle
    hip boots, 140
    knotted leaders, 139-40
    lines, 139-39

lines, 138-39
nets, 140-41
reels, 138
rods, 137-38
waders, 140
This Wonderful World of Trout (Fox),
    13, 20
Tricos, 70
Trout Unlimited, 167

Waders, 140
Wading approach, 156-57
White ants, 63-64
Willow Beetle, 57
Wood, Dick, 24, 105-8
Wulff, Lee, 139

Yarn Inchworm, 120
Yellow Breeches Anglers and
    Conservation Association (YBACA),
    167-68
Yellow-deer-hair clipped-bodied hop-
    per, 85